Bound and Gagged in Hollywood

Edmund L. Hartmann, Screenwriter and Producer

Donald W. McCaffrey

The Scarecrow Press, Inc.
Lanham, Maryland • Toronto • Oxford
2006

SCARECROW PRESS, INC.

Published in the United States of America
by Scarecrow Press, Inc.
A wholly owned subsidiary of
The Rowman & Littlefield Publishing Group, Inc.
4501 Forbes Boulevard, Suite 200, Lanham, Maryland 20706
www.scarecrowpress.com

PO Box 317
Oxford
OX2 9RU, UK

Copyright © 2006 by Donald W. McCaffrey
All rights reserved. No part of this publication may be reproduced, stored in a retrieval system, or transmitted in any form or by any means, electronic, mechanical, photocopying, recording, or otherwise, without the prior permission of the publisher.

British Library Cataloguing in Publication Information Available

Library of Congress Cataloging-in-Publication Data
McCaffrey, Donald W.
 Bound and gagged in Hollywood : Edmund L. Hartmann, screenwriter and producer / Donald W. McCaffrey.
  p. cm.
 Includes bibliographical references and index.
 ISBN-13: 978-0-8108-5729-2 (pbk. : alk. paper)
 ISBN-10: 0-8108-5729-4 (pbk. : alk. paper)
 1. Hartmann, Edmund L., 1911– 2. Screenwriters—United States—Biography. 3. Motion picture producers and directors—United States—Biography. 4. Television writers—United States—Biography. 5. Television producers and directors—United States—Biography. 6. Hollywood (Los Angeles, Calif.)—Biography. I. Title.
PS3515.A7966Z77 2006
808.2'3092—dc22   2005036298

∞™ The paper used in this publication meets the minimum requirements of American National Standard for Information Sciences—Permanence of Paper for Printed Library Materials, ANSI/NISO Z39.48-1992.
Manufactured in the United States of America.

Dedicated to my wife, Joann, who shared the tales of Hollywood from screenwriter Ed Hartmann, and whom he counted, among many other married women, as one of his platonic girlfriends. Ed became Santa Fe's outstanding raconteur and dinner companion.

CONTENTS

FOREWORD	vii
ACKNOWLEDGMENTS	ix
INTRODUCTION—A Recognition of His Talent	1
1 He Wrote for the Stars but Didn't Want to Direct Them	5
2 In the Beginning Hartmann Gave Birth to *Princess Nita*	15
3 Creative Independence at Universal	21
4 Don't Let the Fat Lady Sing: The Writers	27
5 Send in the Clowns	33
6 Thanks for the Memories: There was Hope	47
7 Of Songs, Music Men, and Hartmann	61
8 Bound and Gagged: The Censored and Damned	69
9 Much ado about Family on TV	75
10 Rolling the Final Credits	83
APPENDIXES	93
BIBLIOGRAPHY	103
INDEX	105

FOREWORD
By Edmund Hartmann

Originally my concept of the title of *Bound and Gagged in Hollywood* had one meaning: the fact that in the early 1930s I was Hollywood bound from my spare existence as a writer for Broadway reviews. In California I was hired to create gags plus routines for actors and eventually had total story control as a producer. The author of my career has worked on a meaning to give the title another twist. Like the hero or heroine of the silent days, a writer in Hollywood was bound and gagged to a studio—not to the railroad tracks, of course. As will be seen in this book, attention is certainly paid to the actors and directors. Unfortunately, the contract writer would remain in the background, even though his work is essential, the creative beginning of a successful film drama. A contract writer for even the best studios of the period, MGM and Paramount, became expendable. So, in some sense we were bound and gagged—especially in the age of the blacklisting—the presumed threat of a taboo ideology of Communism in the 1940s and 1950s created havoc in Hollywood. And you will read of the harsh, competitive politics within the system coming from all sides—among writers, directors, producers, and even the star actors. However, there are many pleasant periods of successful pictures that made the creative effort all worthwhile.

I'm certainly indebted to the many interviewers who have shown interest in my career in films and television. The most recent article appears in the October 2003 *Santa Fean* magazine by Rachel Ray. Robert Nott, a theatre and movie critic for the *Santa Fe New Mexican*, has published interviews in this local newspaper and *FilmFax*, a cinema and television magazine. Max Wilk has a book to be published this fall with eleven prominent screenwriters in which I am included. Now, Don McCaffrey has this book fully devoted to an analysis of my works in pictures and television.

October 14, 2003

ACKNOWLEDGMENTS

Since the publication of *Assault on Society: Satirical Literature to Film* in 1992, Christopher Jacobs has been one of the chief creators of my publications as well as being a coauthor of *Guide to the Silent Years of American Cinema*. His role has been that of a proof-editor, idea consultant, and the architect of this camera-ready volume on the prolific screenwriter and producer Edmund L. Hartmann. Another person, Francesca Zorzi, an artist from Switzerland, has assisted with photo composition and research, as she did for *The Road to Comedy: The Films of Bob Hope*.

I am grateful for the supporting views on other critical works of Bob Hope by Jonathan Reichman. He is one of the persons who possess a thorough knowledge of the studies of the comedian's life with a heretofore minimal examination of his films. He contacted me soon after Hartmann's death in early December 2004.

In order to reflect on and evaluate the range of Ed Hartmann's motion picture features, especially the musical comedy films, Leo G. Willette unearthed some seldom-seen films of Hartmann that are analyzed in chapter 7, "Of Songs, Music Men, and Hartmann."

Two events indicate the popularity of Edmund Hartmann in the Santa Fe community: Ed's ninetieth birthday in 2001 and a memorial to his talents as a weaver of anecdotes on his career in films and television. Persons responsible for a salute to his talent were Lynn and Norman Brown, Gordie and George Holloway, Sandy and Russell Osterman, and Anne and Kelly Shannon. This final tribute was held on January 11, 2004.

I'm indebted to theatre and film evaluator Robert Nott and film critic Jon Bowman for published interviews and appraisals of the motion pictures of Edmund Hartmann. Both of them write for the *Santa Fe New Mexican*.

Stephen Ryan, acquisitions editor for Scarecrow Press, has been especially helpful in developing the final concept for the manuscript of this book.

INTRODUCTION
A Recognition of His Talent

Screenwriter-producer Ed Hartmann moved from a back-biting, hubristic Hollywood, a world full of jealous, power-driven battlers, and a meek crowd of the insecure, to the calm world of New Mexico. He found a sanctuary in his retirement, followed by the recognition of his accomplishment from four Santa Fe film critics, the general public, and the New Mexico governor. Also, he found a haven with other filmmakers in the much-touted "land of enchantment," a slogan from the public relations staff in the state capitol. For in this land, first and second homes were purchased by such celebrities as Shirley MacLaine, Gene Hackman, Carol Burnett, Brian Dennehy, Marsha Mason, Jane Fonda, Wes Studi, Ali MacGraw, and Julia Roberts.

Hartmann, I discovered, scripted nearly all genres of films—adventure, mystery, musicals, comedy, and even fantasy. He wrote works for Basil Rathbone, Bob Hope, Abbott and Costello, Martin and Lewis, Jon Hall, Andy Devine, Lucille Ball, Maria Montez, Joan Fontaine, and many others. Turning to television the writer-producer created situation comedies for Eve Arden, Fred MacMurray, William Frawley, William Demarest, Brian Keith, Sebastian Cabot, Nancy Walker, Henry Fonda, Janet Blair, John Forsythe, and Walter Brennan. Consequently, he provided many anecdotes about these and many other stars.

While much of this examination of the art of writer-producer Hartmann could be labeled a history of film and television by the creator, his legacy now appears—not as videos of many of his movies or reruns of his *My Three Sons* or *Family Affair*—but as a revival of his '60s and '70s invention, *Family Affair*. In September 2002, an updated reworking of this situation comedy began. The pilot plus fourteen other episodes graced the 2002-2003 season. So this legacy received a contemporary rebirth.

Edmund received the pilot program, filmed with an entirely new cast and generated on May 5, 2002. The adult cast members are probably the strongest departure from the 1966 pilot, called "Buffy," an initial episode that focuses on the child clinging to the doll she calls Mrs. Beasley. It is a doll she maintains is a real person. The September 2002 version actually borrows most of the content from the original television pilot as conceived and written by Hartmann.

Aired September 12, 1966, Ed's "Buffy" won an award with a concentration on the invasion of the moppet Buffy into Uncle Bill's New York plush apartment. Two other orphans of Bill Davis's brother, Jody and Sissy follow her. The 2002 version employs the humorous frustration of the manservant, Mr. French, as he tries to deal with children. The main change is the character of this manager of the Davis household apartment. Mr. French, as played by comedian Tim Curry, exhibits a greater degree of frustration and consequently more sarcasm than exhibited by the originator of the role, Sebastian Cabot. A character actor and comedian, Curry has many film and television credits that go back to the '70s and '80s. He appeared as the oddball scientist, Doctor Frank-N-Furter, in the so-called classic cult film *The Rocky Horror Show* (1975). Moving more often to the medium of television he played the surly, villainous Bill Sikes to George C. Scott's Fagin in an adaptation of the novel by Charles Dickens, *Oliver Twist* (1982). Also more tied to the medium of TV, Gary Cole, who played the father in the 1995 *Brady Bunch Movie,* plays the role of Uncle Bill Davis in the new version of *Family Affair.*

Both lead adult actors, Curry and Cole, possess impressive credits in comedies made for the media of movies and television. Ed Hartmann lent me a tape of the 2002 pilot and wondered if I thought the show would have the lasting quality of his '60s into '70s production. From the revision pilot, I said, it depends if the situation comedy maintains the same high standards of writing, acting, and directing. Even with the recent nostalgic movement to revisit and refurbish past film and television works, the taste of the public may be erratic. Checking the websites of both Tim Curry and Gary Cole proved fruitful. Both actors have an impressive following of fans. Evidently the Warner Brothers network realized this and pushed the *Family Affair* sitcom. Enthusiastic website editor Christine Zachman reported with the abundant use of rhapsodic exclamation marks:

> Commercials are now airing on WB for the fall season! Also, the WB website has 2 small clips from the show, both featuring Tim as Mr. French. WB has officially set "Family Affair" to air on Thursday nights! . . . The people at WB say that they are willing to give this series a few seasons to establish itself!

If the faith Warner Brothers invested in the eventual success of the program held, Hartmann would have been very happy. He said, "I hope it continues like my series. It gives me money." And that is not merely a mercenary statement. As contract writer-producer for CBS he never received the recognition and financial reward he deserved. In an ironic footnote to his long career, the honor and legacy arrived for his golden years of retirement here in Santa Fe, miles and a culture away from Hollywood. But it would not be as fulfilling as it might have been. The updated *Family Affair* folded before it might have been renewed for a second season. "They didn't know what to do with it," Ed reflected after he had witnessed a number of the contemporary episodes.

Since Ed had written seven films for Bob Hope, he must have taken on the skill of the famous comedian to handle one-liner quips. And he found one of the joys of a life of ninety years emerged by a steady banter with me, the interviewer. Of course I was outclassed when he found that research for two years might be necessary. "I might be dead by that time." Ed said. "So might I," came my reply. With only a beat, he came back with, "We will just have to concentrate on living."

While Hartmann was disappointed that the resurrection of *Family Affair* was short-lived, he could live on his laurels. His screenplays for Bob Hope displayed his exceptional skills at the height of his motion picture career.

1
He Wrote for the Stars but Didn't Want to Direct Them

Asked why he didn't become a director in Hollywood like several of his colleagues who were coscreenwriters, Hartmann replied that he didn't want to deal daily with actors. However, he found that some actors were gracious and respected the skills of the writers who provided their scripts. Some seemed too aloof and self-centered to the point that they ignored or even looked down on Hartmann and his colleagues. His collaborator, Hal Kanter, shared Ed's admiration for Bob Hope. Hope exhibited respect for the scribes who gave him material for his films, radio, and television shows. He was friendly and went out of his way to greet them whenever he saw them—at social events and even on the street. Hartmann told me that he knew only one lapse in the graciousness of Hope. The actor had a battery of script and gag writers. He prepared to hand out the checks for this group. Standing on a balcony above them, he tossed the checks to them as if scattering pennies to children. But this crude joke backfired. One writer recovered his check and dramatically tore it up before his colleagues and Hope. It was atypical of Bob—more like a prank expected from Jerry Lewis.

Ed and Hal Kanter seemed to share a dislike for Jerry Lewis. Hal, in his autobiography on show business, *So Far, So Funny,* characterized Lewis's idea of practical jokes as a "junior grade sadist," (McFarland, p. 153). Evidently Jerry had not graduated from the class clown—and there is evidence that even in his mature years he remained egocentric. Edmund relates how Lewis pretended to want Dean Martin to have his "best picture" when he talked to the writers who handled the script for *The Caddy.* According to Hartmann, Lewis made sure he became the center of the film. "Well," Ed concluded, "By the time we finished the script, Dean Martin had hardly anything to do in the film at all, thanks to Lewis."

The comedian who became famous for his ability to handle light or romantic humor was the type of personality that blended best with the urbane Hartmann's personality. Hope, who could do some slapstick, had the personal demeanor of an English gentleman. So, Ed indicated, he would spend time giving the concept of the script to Bob for his approval, and he seemed to reject very little of the plot and gags the screenwriter suggested. Of course, Hartmann eventually handled some of the best light comedians in his successful years as a television producer and writer. He found sympathetic relationships with Fred MacMurray, Sebastian Cabot, Henry Fonda, Brian Keith, and John Forsythe. During the '60s into the '70s, CBS television gave Hartmann total control. He admitted that he enjoyed this more than his Hollywood days when he was a contract writer and producer.

When Ed wrote for Paramount in the '40s, he encountered enough problems with actors that he didn't move to directing as some of his associate writers did. Hartmann gave an example of how he went out of his way to write a skit for Alan Ladd and William Bendix. It was for a benefit stage presentation that was similar to the 1947 film *Variety Girl,* and featured almost the whole gamut of Paramount stars and minor actors. With some important major contract actors, over a hundred of the studio players cluttered this potpourri film. Such notable talents were used as an audience attraction: Bob Hope, Bing Crosby, Gary Cooper, Ray Milland, Barbara Stanwyck, Dorothy Lamour, William Holden, and Burt Lancaster. Of course, these big names made only cameo appearances. Hartmann wrote a comic script for the stage benefit presented by the Variety Clubs International that focused on a humorous altercation between Ladd and Bendix. Edmund even took the time to rehearse the sketch with them. It was an extensive amount of time for Hartmann and he was taking over the role of a director. When I realized this might provide a change and move for his career, I asked him why he didn't become a director. "I didn't want to spend my day with them." And, except for a few big names like Bob Hope, the screenwriter spent minimal time with actors. As a Hollywood contract writer, Ed had more contact with the director or producer. His most direct disenchantment with actors occurred when he wrote and produced for the teams of Abbott and Costello, Olsen and Johnson, plus just one script for the Ritz Brothers. Hartmann experienced his difficulty with actors in these writing and producing days. It was obvious why he did not want to move to the position of director for such wacky characters.

A reflection by Hartmann on Bud Abbott and Lou Costello appears in television interviews and private interviews I had with him. He indicated to me that a strained relationship existed between the long-term burlesque comics. It was more than unfriendly. "They hated each other," Ed said. One time Bud wound up to give a slapstick punch to Lou. Costello staggered backward from a blow that connected and hurt. On the other hand, the chubby member of the comedy team could deliver psychological pain. He convinced studio heads that he was the important part of the duo that delivered the laughs. He wanted more money. To rub it in he showed the latest check to the crew on the set to prove he was the king of comedy—highly superior to his colleague, Bud Abbott. This was the Mr. Hyde part of Lou.

The kindly Dr. Jekyll emerged when Costello, who was nearly a child himself, met a moppet, Susan Hartmann, the writer-producer's daughter. Lou stopped the shooting of scenes to ride her around in a motorized vehicle and show her sights in the studio lot. The comedian invited Edmund and his wife to his house. While this seemed to be an amiable gesture, they witnessed an odd dwelling and an odd host. They went through room after room of additions. "It was like a train," Ed recalled. When they got to the caboose, there was a bar and a place for a drink. Two women, hookers, sat at a table nearby. Lou didn't introduce his friends.

The straight man of the Abbott and Costello team, Bud, was not the colorful character of his partner. Unfortunately he had a physical problem that increased production costs. In the middle of shooting a scene a man designated to watch him would call for a break. Abbott periodically would have an epileptic seizure.

While producing two films for the Olsen and Johnson comedy team, *Ghost Catchers* (1944) and *See My Lawyer* (1945), Hartmann found out this pair had a physical problem—that of age. Famous for the stage and film version of *Hellzapoppin'*, put on the screen in 1941, they were no longer what could be called "hot property." Chic Johnson's slipping dentures proved to be another production problem. "He had all kinds of false teeth," Ed told me, "And none of them fit. In the middle of a scene he would unconsciously pull the teeth out and shake them in the air. Sometimes we would catch this when we looked at the rushes. If we couldn't cut this out, we had to reshoot the scene."

But even more of a problem was the fact that Hartmann was also producing and writing for the studio's "hot property," Bud Abbott and Lou Costello. Olsen and Johnson, on the other hand, had become a passe comedy duo. To the producer Hartmann's consternation, a theatre screening of *Ghost Chasers* brought the ultimate audience rejection. The crowd thought it would be seeing an Abbott and Costello comedy. When the opening credits, "Olsen and Johnson" appeared, the aisle filled to the brim and only a few people remained to see the once famous theatre team in their latest movie. Obviously, Olsen and Johnson had had their day in the sun many years ago. They started in vaudeville in 1918 while Abbott and Costello had arrived as a team in 1936 and the transition to film in the '40s met with outstanding success. But even Bud and Lou's fortunes would fade in a very short time. With their pictures resting on such "Meet" films as *Abbott & Costello Meet Frankenstein* (1948), *Abbott & Costello Meet the Killer, Boris Karloff* (1949), and into the '50s with encounters with the Invisible Man, Captain Kidd, Dr. Jekyll and Mr. Hyde, Keystone Kops, and the Mummy obviously they were grinding out odd fare. In only a few short years after Hartmann wrote and produced the effective works *Naughty Nineties* and *In Society* there was a steady degeneration of the team's movies. They would break up in 1957. Both Lou and Bud sank into debt after making enough money to keep them for their life. They were has-beens. Edmund was fortunate to be the basic creator during their heyday.

Before a threesome comedy group retired from movies in 1943, Hartmann wrote one of four scripts at Universal created for the wackiest team from vaudeville, the Ritz Brothers. While they were far down the critical chart by evaluators, they managed some of the silliness of routines that the Marx Brothers executed with unusual aplomb. Brash overplaying marked the Ritz Brothers's style. Ed wrote solo the 1943 *Hi 'ya Chum,* one of the oddest titles for any movie. "I didn't tell my friends I was writing a script for them," Ed told me. Not everyone liked their brand of humor, but Hartmann agreed with me that this group was many degrees above the comedy of the Three Stooges. And, both groups had their fans. As actors he knew during the creation of the movie, the screenwriter-producer liked the Ritz Brothers as persons more than any comedy team he scripted for.

One of the most famous stars from the '30s and '40s, Fred MacMurray, appeared in the long-running situation comedy, *My Three Sons.* Hartmann, as producer and writer for the series, found the actor the opposite of the Olsen and Johnson team. Not only was he ageless, he possessed a consistency and a skill to handle any assignment. In his long Hollywood career, he appeared in musicals, light comedy, and serious dramas. His first starring role was with Katharine Hepburn in the 1935 *Alice Adams* and the next important work *Trail of the Lonesome Pine* (1936), with Henry Fonda. While Fred never won an Oscar he received a Best Actor Award for the film noir work *Double Indemnity* (1944) by the New York Film Critics Circle.

Since he acted in many other important motion pictures, his professional abilities were well developed and can be called unique. In his work for television he could do scenes as if other actors were present—as he played before a camera all by himself. Assignments made it economical to use Fred for a limited time and the entire cast of *My Three Sons* at another time. Radio actors of decades ago had such skills as they created "cloud topped towers" in their minds. Such ingenuity and the imagination was, of course, rare in the late '50s and '70s and seemed to be possessed mostly by older actors and actresses who graduated from vaudeville, the so-called legitimate theatre, and radio. Fred MacMurray had at least one outstanding eccentricity. Being a well-paid actor, his actions prompted Hartmann to wonder if he were still living in the Great Depression of the '30s. Way past Easter, Fred brought his lunch and peeled the shell from a colored, boiled egg. The parsimonious performer sighed, "Well, this is the last one."

MacMurray played the leading role of Steve Douglas in the situation comedy, *My Three Sons,* for twelve years, one of the most successful comedies for the medium.

Edmund Hartmann had some of the demure, southern quality that probably explained his affinity with British actors, Basil Rathbone and Sebastian Cabot. Screenwriter Hal Kanter wrote in his autobiography that Ed was "a soft-spoken, literate gentleman and one of the wittiest it has been my good fortune to know" (from *So Far, So Funny,* p. 151). These traits indicate why Hartmann could, as a writer, associate easily with not only the leading actors and actresses but with other creative talents as well in the production line of filmmaking. This interviewer revealed that he had somewhat negative contacts with Rathbone at the Hollywood Hotel and at one of his engagements performing a single's act with Shakespeare monologues. "I found him aloof and even surly," I said. Ed replied that he had only positive memories of his contact with Basil when he penned

Sherlock Holmes and the Secret Weapon (1942) and *The Scarlet Claw* (1944). My contacts were in the '60s when Rathbone's career was on the decline. After a rather successful spoof of the horror genre, *Comedy of Terrors,* in 1964, the actor appeared in such odd fare as *Voyage to the Prehistoric Planet* (1965), *The Ghost in the Invisible Bikini* (1966), and *Hillbillies in a Haunted House* (1967). Rathbone became a parody of his intense, sometimes mannered but always authoritative, style of acting. Again, Ed was fortunate to write for an actor when he was a leading star in the Sherlock Holmes series for Universal.

Hartmann's scripts in the '30s for RKO and Universal Studios focused on crime and adventure melodramas with heroes and villains as the leading persona. Basil Rathbone played heroes such as his Sherlock Holmes and villains such as his Sir Guy of Gisborne in *The Adventures of Robin Hood* in 1938. Rathbone could be said to be an important character actor—that is, a dramatic artist who plays a range of roles that are deviations from the standard leading role.

Ed scripted for a more conventional hero in one of the leading men for Universal in the '40s and '50s, Jon Hall. He was, in a way, the studio's challenge to Errol Flynn, an idol of young boys between the ages of nine and eleven years who played games of being a swashbuckling protagonist after seeing *The Adventures of Robin Hood.*

Jon Hall proved to be a handsome lead like Flynn when he reached stardom with John Ford's four-star rated *The Hurricane* in 1937. He portrayed an abused native lad on a South Seas island with the attire that almost matched the Johnny Weissmuller loincloth of the Tarzan movies of the '30s. In Hartmann's solo scripted *Ali Baba and the Forty Thieves* (1943) Hall could not show his muscles since his role was a type of Arabian character, Ali, who had to be draped for the desert sun.

Ed recalls that Jon Hall came from a physical exam that meant that he would not have to enter the military during the draft of World War II. "He sat back in a chair," his screenwriter said, "and with relief said, 'At last, I can act.'" There was a surprising number of reasons for deferment from serving in the war at that time. Many of them physical. Some of the heroes of the movies kept their psychological or physical deficiency for not serving quiet. And the press obliged, unlike the vultures of the press today. Mentally incompetent men and homosexual men could avoid the draft. Also the myopic, heart defective, and physically handicapped were some of those commonly deferred from service. Some people wondered why such physically active men on the screen, with healthy looks and the muscular development of Atlas could be rejected for service in a very popular war effort. However, to the public the screen heroes were something like the Greek gods. They had achieved mythical status and were not of our world. Jon Hall enjoyed his limited fame without reproach.

Not so, another swashbuckler, Errol Flynn. The masculinity of this dashing screen lead seemed to be carried over in his personal affairs. Errol developed a reputation as a man who would lust after anything that moved. One of his affairs developed a saying "In like Flynn"—to indicate a sexual conquest.

Unlike Hall, the actor Flynn who also specialized in adventure films would have preferred to serve in the real-life world of the war instead of a fictional depiction of the conflict like the 1945 *Objective, Burma!* Errol had a number of physical problems that prevented him from such a dream: a weak heart, periodic reoccurring malaria attacks, and tuberculosis.

While Hartmann did not write for that idol of the adventure movie, he related an incident of an attempted conquest going awry. Errol became a victim of a wag who set him up. Knowing well of this star's overactive testosterone, he was told of a beautiful actress who would willingly fall on her back if her breasts were stroked. When Flynn cornered her, he followed the instructions of the mischief-maker. With an Amazon's strength and fury, she hauled off a right fist smack to his mouth, breaking front teeth. Production on a film starring Errol had to be delayed for several weeks until his face would be presentable. This certainly punctured the myth of "In like Flynn."

Hartmann found out that actresses could engage in mischief. Who would have thought that one of the seemingly reserved sisters, Olivia de Havilland and Joan Fontaine, could be a trickster. Born Joan de Beauvoir de Havilland, the woman who took the name of Fontaine tried to shake the reserve of Edmund. During the shooting of the 1953 *Casanova's Big Night* with Bob Hope, she invited Hartmann for a card game. Hartmann had scripted the movie with Hal Kanter and wanted to be obliging. When he was dealt a hand, the sight inwardly shocked him. It was a deck with a series of pornographic photos with some raw depictions. "I continued the game as if nothing was different from the ordinary," Ed told me. Fontaine failed with the unflappable Hartmann. Actually, *Casanova's Big Night* provided a vehicle for Joan that displayed a feisty side of her nature. It remains one of her best comedies.

Even a prop man in Hollywood could play a practical joke. And it was a forceful one that conditioned the siren actress Maria Montez. She had a dressing tent for the shooting of the 1943 *Ali Baba and the Forty Thieves*. According to Hartmann she could have walked 50 yards for a rest room. "But she was the type of person who wasn't about to walk 50 yards, especially if she was in a hurry. So she would just urinate on the tent floor and let the prop man clean it up." (From Robert Nott's interview in the *Santa Fe New Mexican*, Friday, August 12, p. 62.) Evidently the prop man got tired of what Hartmann characterized as "shabby" behavior. He placed some carbide powder used to set off explosives in the floor of the tent where Montez relieved herself.

Ed explained the results of the trap: "The mixture would explode if it came into contact with water. So after she went into her tent we all waited. And suddenly 'Wham!' goes the tent and Montez comes out screaming. Needless to say, after that she didn't mind walking the 50 yards to the toilet" (Nott, p. 62).

Edmund told me this incident and another eccentricity about Maria. She would walk into the Paramount cafeteria that advertised a place where the public could see the stars. In she strolled with a see-through dress, looking for attention—not from the fans but executives, in order to further her career. If she saw no one of any importance from management, she would turn around and walk out.

While Montez dealt in spectacle, Bud Abbott and Lou Costello touted their presence with sight and sound. A group of cronies surrounded them and one of them beat a drum. The entrance eventually grew and was accompanied by something akin to a band. This came about when they realized they had become one of the most important comedy teams in Hollywood. Before that rise to fame they would come unobtrusively into the commissary and sit in a corner.

Lucille Ball didn't possess the same quirks that Maria Montez had, except that as she became better known and successful, she had a tendency to insist on flaunting her celebrity status. Nearly stumbling during two phases of her career, she posed nude and registered as a communist. However, she would prevail. As screenwriter, Ed wrote three movies for Miss Ball and found her to be a likeable and charming person. In the early '30s she was a model who wasn't reluctant to pose in the buff. She also seemed to be without clothes as she appeared briefly as a slave woman in Eddie Cantor's *Roman Scandals* (1933). Very long tresses covered her attractive body so that a person's imagination had to fill in the details. Since she was an unknown with a small niche in Hollywood, she did not suffer rejection by the public. However, it was entirely different when the House Un-American Activities Committee discovered a left leaning patriarch in her family. When she was young and innocent her grandfather talked her into registering as a communist. The dredging up the past by the committee was at the height of her television career in the '50s when she was leading comedienne of situation comedy with her popular *I Love Lucy*. She thought it would ruin her career. However, while the committee more often pushed to prove the innocent person guilty, the members of the group really loved Lucy and wanted to forgive her. She easily got off the hook.

Edmund's scripts for Miss Ball were not the simplistic humor and often slapstick affairs of the sitcom *I Love Lucy*. In fact, her first important role for motion picture was a serious, sophisticated story of a woman who was successful as the executive of a cosmetic business of her own invention. It was a vehicle called *Beauty for the Asking* (1939). By 1949 Ball had appeared in a number of pictures, but Ed said that she became "box office poison." "Producers and directors did not hire her," Hartmann indicated, "But Hope wanted her anyway and gave her the chance she needed." And the Damon Runyon adaptation, *Sorrowful Jones* in 1949 proved her an excellent companion for Bob Hope, who was at the pinnacle of his career. As Hope's girlfriend, Lucille held her own without traits of a wacky character or the features of an airhead. Instead, she displayed a type of detached wit that proved the comedienne could turn a line with Hope.

When Miss Ball costarred with Hope in a film released a year later, in 1950, *Fancy Pants*, she emerged as a much lighter comic character without some of the sharp, cutting remarks she delivered in her previous pairing with Hope. *Fancy Pants,* a much different work than a Runyon story, became a successful remake of the 1935 *Ruggles of Red Gap*. Writers Hartmann and Robert O'Brien created a broader comedy than they created for *Sorrowful Jones.*

While Lucille Ball posed in the nude for still photos, Hedy Lamarr took off her clothes for a movie, *Ecstasy* (1933). In the formative age of the medium nudity existed, usually sneaked in with long shots to show degeneration of a past civilization—especially in some silent epics by D. W. Griffith and Cecil B. De

Mille. However, scandals in the early '20s resulted in the Hays Office regulating the motion picture industry—in short, developing moral guidelines. But *Ecstasy* was a foreign film and slipped by the censors as one of the '30s sexploitation movies. One of the most outstanding brunette beauties of cinema appeared swimming without a bathing suit, running through the woods with full frontal nudity. In a climactic scene, in the story and for the woman, Lamarr moves in ecstasy with a close headshot for a poetic, soft-core seduction. It is a scene created with excellent taste and one that is merely erotic.

Evidently MGM thought Hedy would look almost as beautiful clothed as she did in those *Ecstasy* scenes. And she was. When she took a role for the Paramount Studio, Hartmann cowrote the Bob Hope vehicle *My Favorite Spy* (1951). He indicated that he created a more important part when she served as a romantic interest for Hope. However, Lamarr actually became a victim of her own beauty. In many ways she became the kind of woman used by comedians from the silent days of the ladies used by Charles Chaplin, Harold Lloyd, and Buster Keaton. They were "straight women" for the comedian, with some possibilities of a romantic conclusion. Lamarr was one of several women to play opposite Hope in a series of films: *My Favorite Blonde* (1942) with Madeleine Carroll, and *My Favorite Brunette* (1947) with Dorothy Lamour. And, of course, these women filled the role of romantic interest for the lead, comedian Bob Hope. Hedy Lamarr seldom was able to show her skills as an actress. She appeared in a number of roles as a sexual woman in such 1942 movies as *White Cargo* and *Tortilla Flat*, and was the ultimate femme fatale in *Samson and Delilah* (1949).

Hartmann cowrote another Hedy Lamarr movie, *Let's Live a Little* (1945), that gave her a solid feminist role of a lovely psychiatrist who wrote a number of books on her expertise. She portrayed a cool beauty who was an intellectual. And while this romantic comedy was typical of the period, Hedy, at last, had a part to fit her total qualifications. It has been reported that she possessed a marvelous brain that was as exceptional as her beautiful face and body.

But with *Let's Live a Little*, Ed got Robert Cummings as a leading man and a producer. The actor had a history of eccentric approaches to his career. When he wanted to be an actor on the stage in New York, he tried to pass himself off as British. Then, as a person born in Joplin, Missouri, he tried to affect the character of a Texan when he went to Hollywood. With a birth name that stretched the continent, Charles Clarence Robert Orville Cummings, his credits were sometimes listed as Blade Stanhope Conway and Bruce Hutchens.

Here was one actor that annoyed screenwriter Ed Hartmann more than most men that he was associated with while scripting a film. Edmund told me that he liked to do "sophisticated pictures" and Cummings wanted to change the plot and his character of the 1948 *Let's Live a Little* in wacky ways. Since Bob had invested money in this picture, he wanted to call the shots. He declared that he wanted to have a Loch Ness monster in this movie with the name of Oscar. Asked why he wanted this discordant aspect in a plot that was not in Scotland, Cummings indicated that it was intended as a poke at his lawyer whom he disliked and whose name was Oscar. Furthermore, the actor thought that in order to be humorous, the character he was to enact must be changed from public relations person to a "ceramics engineer." Cummings wanted this odd euphemism because the word toilet would not be proper to use in a movie. Ed was baffled by these requests and was perceptive enough to know that here was an actor who was so fey that his mind must have existed on some place in space. So, this actor might not realize that Hartmann would ignore his suggestions even if he were a producer. Ed concluded with a civil understatement, "He was a strange man."

While my wife, Joann, and I were having a pleasant Italian dinner at a local restaurant with our host, Edmund Hartmann, I asked the writer-producer if he had ever acted.

"When we were at the end of shooting and production had shut down, I took a part by necessity. As producer of the television series, I was the only one available. Had the make-up man fix me up as an old man. Shot it with some children."

"What series was it?" I asked.

"*Family Affair.*"

As a writer who liked to remain at the typewriter and didn't want to spend his day directing actors, this intrigued me so that I had to ask: "This was the only time you acted?"

"The only time."

Since I had a number of interviews with Hartmann, I knew he did have some favorite actors. He didn't see them as pawns for writers, directors, and producers, or spoiled, self-centered people who ignored all other creators in the industry.

I had forgot, of course, his favorite, and wanted to hear again who it was.

"I liked my association with Fred MacMurray," he said.

"And Bob Hope, I recall."

"Of course."

And he followed up with his admiration of Basil Rathbone.

He really did want to share his day with these actors.

2
In the Beginning Hartmann Gave Birth to *Princess Nita*

Ed handed me a thin book with the title *Princess Nita*—book, lyrics & music by Edmund Hartmann. The cover displayed a woman in royal Egyptian raiment with a desert and the Sphinx in the background. Highly stylized, there appeared an art deco motif and also within the drawing a panel that listed ten songs—the contents of the booklet.

"At the university this musical usually had three people handling each aspect of the production. I did everything: the book, lyrics, and music."

I found this memento from the past intriguing. Here was the key to Ed's whole professional life that spanned five decades. *Princess Nita* became the springboard for a young creator at Washington University in St. Louis.

Ed explained, "I had no intention to go to Hollywood. I was from St. Louis and wanted to go to New York to create musicals."

Obviously, he was a prodigy. Not yet out of his teens, he already had command of storytelling plus musical skill that would be applied in his future occupation as a screenwriter and producer.

In New York Hartmann started on songs and sketches for a forthcoming "George White's Scandals." This project didn't materialize because the money couldn't be raised for the show. However, Jack Yellen, a songwriter Ed worked with, moved to Hollywood and put in a good word that changed Ed's career. Yellen had achieved success as a songwriter, composer, and screenwriter for Fox, creating in 1934 *George White's Scandals*. Later he would become the leading songsmith and screenwriter for Fox's sensational moppet star, Shirley Temple.

Hartmann believed himself a failure at that time.

"I thought I would never make it on Broadway and I called my father to get bus money to go back to St. Louis. I was alone in my apartment. The phone rang. 'This is Hunter Lovelace, head of Fox Studios story department in New York. We'd like you to go to Hollywood and be a writer. How much would you take?' Now I was getting fifteen dollars a week as a reader of possible stage material for the Shuberts's production company. I don't know why I answered like this. Impulsively I said three hundred dollars a week. He laughed. 'You've never done a picture. You have no credits. We can't pay you that.' There was a pause. He said, 'Would you take two fifty?' I'd never seen two hundred and fifty dollars in my life. Anyway, that got me out to Hollywood."

Edmund L. Hartmann's introduction to Tinsel Town would be even more incredible—something akin to a surrealistic dream.

"I was in the Fox writers' building and had an office. Nothing happened for a week. I kept waiting for them to tell me what to do and where to go."

In one of his colorful monologues Ed continued to describe an event that became a wild goose chase.

The phone rang and he was asked to be out in front of the writers' building in five minutes. "I'll be out in four," Ed replied. A car carried him for an hour's drive to the Gas Building in Long Beach.

"We arrived." Ed continued his narration as if his introduction to Hollywood had happened yesterday. "I don't know anything we're doing. Don't know the picture. I don't know anything."

The future screenwriter found himself pulled toward a tall building and up the stairs to a room with a set of huge dynamos of the Gas and Electric Company. There a barbershop set had been constructed in this unlikely location. And the oddest barber appeared, Stepin Fetchit, a black comedian of the '30s whose lines came out as if he had a mouth full of mush. Ed got introduced to the director, Henry King, creator of such famous works as *Tol'able David* (1921), *In Old Chicago* (1938), *Twelve O'Clock High* (1949), *The Song of Bernadette* (1943), and many other critically acclaimed movies. The film production was taking place in the early '30s, and when it would finally be released *Marie Galante* would receive kudos for the director. Director King pulled Ed aside and gave him an assignment: "You are to write some funny lines for Stepin Fetchit."

Hartmann sighed as he recalled this task: "To write lines for him would be dialogue no one would understand anyway."

On a spent envelope of an old letter Ed tried to write lines on the spot. Not much would come of this first test as a screenwriter; however, director King would take the fledgling under his wing and give him a ride to his apartment. He would also become privy to the fate of the 1934 *Marie Galante*, starring Spencer Tracy.

Few would know why, but all production stopped on the picture.

Appearing at the studio the morning after his bizarre introduction to his future profession, Ed learned that the shutdown on the production resulted because the lead, Tracy was missing and no one knew where he was.

Weeks went by and Edmund waited to continue working for Fox. He saw Henry King in the commissary and asked him about Spencer Tracy.

"We found Tracy," King explained. "We found him in New York on a wild drunk. Knockout drops were put in his drink and then he was carried onto a plane and we had him flown back to Hollywood. On the way he came to and went crazy. The copilot knocked him out with a monkey wrench."

Henry faced Spencer, and while King ordinarily was a gentleman, he chewed out the recalcitrant, "You dirty son-of-a-bitch. You ruined the lives of everyone on the picture. We had to fire them until we could start up again."

Ed continued with the fate of the actor: "He was fined in the tens of thousand dollars and his contract was torn up. But he had to finish the picture."

Ironically, *Marie Galante* now is considered a four-star motion picture. And, Tracy soon received a contract from MGM. As a result, by some quirk of fate or good casting, he became an even bigger star. Ten Oscar nominations for a Best Actor greeted Spencer from the '30s to the '50s with two Academy Awards for *Captains Courageous* (1937) and *Boys Town* (1938).

Hartmann, however, had been left hanging on a tether by Fox. The initial open-arms embrace by the industry dissolved into a hands-off or pure neglect. The future Hollywood film author had struggled in vain to produce dialogue for Stepin Fetchit. With a shred of evidence, a scholar for the American Film Institute discovered Ed as a "supporting writer" who contributed to the 1934 *Marie Galante* (*American Film Institute Catalogue, 1931-1940*, p. 1325). In a brief phone interview Hartmann reported, "I worked only one day on the picture. The next day it was closed down. They didn't use my contribution."

Neglect by Fox continued. Ephraim Katz's *Film Encyclopedia* gave Ed credit for the Western *Helldorado* (1934), but the fledgling screenwriter claimed that although he was assigned the picture, he was placed in limbo and never wrote a line for the film.

Months went by and the St. Louis born would-be writer eventually achieved success in the motion picture industry. Ed indicated he wrote many pictures that would never be produced, and I indicated that I, too, know of many projects in the writing phase that today will never be realized for a variety of reasons. "Do you think this happened even more in your days in the '30s?" I asked. He answered: "Many more." Hartman was engaged as a contract writer for the production of low-budget adventure, mystery, and crime films that appealed to audiences of all ages. All phases of production from the screenplay to the finished edited movie had to be accelerated. As a result, an assistant to the producer might make a hasty judgment of the script that led to rejection with little consideration of the screenplay's merit.

Finally, his first assignment to receive a screen credit saw the light of day when Warner Brothers released *The Big Noise* on June 22, 1936. The production on this picture was started in February of that year and Hartmann had sold the story to the company and ironically got a credit under a garbled first name and a misspelled last name: "Edward Hartman."

The Big Noise related the fortunes of a big business protagonist who lost his CEO position by a company board that did not like his way of running the business. Through a number of trials, a small businessman reveals his mettle. Eventually he regains his old position as head of a woolen mill. This upbeat ending after difficulties might have served as a parallel to Edmund Hartmann's struggle in Hollywood as he sometimes became figuratively "bound and gagged" as a contract writer.

As a chronicler of the Hartmann legacy, I noted that bitterness would sometimes creep into the voice of this usually cheerful raconteur. He would more often graciously spin anecdotes on his screenwriting position: his relationship with actors, and his role as a producer. A negative incident would be followed by, "That's Hollywood." For example, he told how after a premier a group would fawn over a creator's picture with words of praise. When the filmmaker left the group the hypocrites would agree with one person's remark: "It's horseshit."

Before he was popular enough to receive backbiting remarks from associates, Edmund became a contract writer for RKO from 1936 to 1939. He created eight produced scripts, most of them crime and adventure dramas. His first co-screenplay in 1936, *Without Orders,* proved that he would make money for the film company. According to Ed, this aviation adventure film became a hit and must have been a precursor of all those near disaster melodramas popularized over a generation later with the successful *Airport* (1970). In *Without Orders* a pilot, faced with a possible crash, abandons his airliner by parachute, leaving no one to fly the plane. From the airport, the hero of the film instructs a stewardess, his girlfriend, how to bring the plane in for a landing. While this may seem overly melodramatic by modern standards, this climactic scene evolved into serving as nearly the total film in many of the '70s successors. The plots were very similar and often more contrived than in this original and innovative prototype.

Possibly following the success of *Without Orders,* Hartmann cowrote a 1937 film, *The Man Who Found Himself,* with a combination of aviation and medical story lines. However, four of his films followed the genre of the crime movies that were so popular in the '30s: *Wanted! Jane Turner* (1936), a crime investigation headed by postal inspectors; *Behind the Headlines* (1937), starring Lee Tracy as a radio reporter who scoops newspapers as he reports crimes; *Hideaway* (1937), a comedy with big city gangsters fleeing the police and attempting to adjust to the ways of a rural community; and *Law of the Underworld* (1937), a melodrama of gangsters involving an innocent couple with a jewelry robbery in New York.

Two works Hartmann wrote for RKO show a strong deviation from the popular crime drama of the period. In the 1937 *China Passage,* Americans get involved in Oriental intrigue with dangerous incidents and a mystery. More important than this adventure film is the 1939 *Beauty for the Asking* with Lucille Ball. A serious drama that had some character delineations much like those that were witnessed in the sophisticated comedy of the period, it displayed a strong feminist touch. In fact Edmund would develop a sophisticated comedy story two years later called *The Feminine Touch* (1941). *Beauty for the Asking* probably evolved from a life example of the woman entrepreneur of the cosmetic industry, Helena Rubenstein. In this fictional depiction, a beautician, Jean Russell (Ms. Ball's role), creates a facial cream that blossoms into a lucrative company. Earlier in her career a cosmetic salesman jilts her, but eventually she not only achieves riches, she also finds her mate. The plot line is obviously one that follows the popular fiction of the day. However it has the twist of a woman who becomes an executive in the business world, a rarer phenomenon in the '30s than it would be today. Hartman punctuated another important fact: "We gave Lucille her first leading role."

When RKO gave Ed fewer assignments and tried to cut down on his overall salary per picture, he made a fortuitous move to Universal where he would eventually be able to produce movies as well as write them. But there were some problems that developed, as interviewer Robert Nott learned from the screenwriter:

> After RKO let me go, I worked at Universal for "The Crime Club" unit which made a series of films based on the mystery books and starred such actors as Preston Foster and Frank Jenks. They were pretty good. I wrote one screenplay in two weeks, and they shot it pretty much as it was! After that I wrote *The Last Warning* (1938) in two weeks, and they felt they really had something in me. But there was this producer—what a prick—who would come into my office and stand over my typewriter and pull the pages out as I wrote them.

Ed Hartmann's talent sometimes became a double-edged sword. Producers wanted to save money and production cost could be cut with a writer who was a fast study dealing with an adaptation plus a creator who delivered a script in a couple of weeks. However, he sometimes was too skilled in delivering scripts that the studio wouldn't need for that year. Producers might cut his weekly salary to a payment by each script. That way they could control the output. And, of course, not pay him as much.

With this move to Universal he would leave behind a collaborator with whom he created five adventure and crime films: *Without Orders, China Passage, The Man Who Found Himself, Hideaway,* and *Behind the Headlines.* The writer was J. Robert Bren, who continued authoring similar films. Before a more positive switch in the genre specialty Ed would still be handling crime and adventure fare for Universal.

Before he received a continuous cowriter, Edmund adapted a play with the playwright Sam Robins and his drama *Enemy Agent* (1940). This work brought kudos from the *New York Times*, a newspaper that routinely reviewed most of the screenwriter's creations because the genres he specialized in were audience pleasers.

> *Enemy Agent* is considerably more entertaining than the average melodrama of this sort. First, the story is told with dispatch; second, and even more important, it has one of the strangest denouements that you are likely to see in a long time—a scene so ludicrously funny that it alone is almost worth the price of admission. Here's a rough idea of what it is like: G-men, masquerading as college boys on a bender, barge into the spy head's home and turn his parlor into a gridiron. When the spy's henchmen come on the run to investigate the racket the G-men down them with flying tackles. (p. 13, April 22, 1940)

Soon Hartmann would be moving to a film that would be totally in the comic mode.

The new Universal collaborator, Stanley Crea Rubin, helped write *Diamond Frontier* and *South to Karanga* for a 1940 release and *San Francisco Docks* a year later. Rubin would become a producer soon after his assignments as a writer and Ed would also take on this same role in the development of musical comedies and humorous works featuring leading comedians in the '40s and '50s. Asked why he took this direction, he informed me, "I received more money for comedies."

The transition to big budget and popular fare can be detected in two variety pictures: *Ma, He's Making Eyes at Me* (1940) and *Time Out for Rhythm* (1941). One of the *New York Times* long-term film critics, Bosley Crowther, gave some recognition of these movies but his appraisal of the films is lukewarm. He gives more attention to the 1941 work. A Columbia Pictures release, the film has "grand hotel" cast of Ann Miller, Rudy Vallee, Rosemary Lane, Allen Jenkins, and The Three Stooges--a typical pattern of the variety show of the early '40s. Crowther gives the best notice to the lead: "Miss Miller, when she sings or dances, does so charmingly and with ease." (p. 16, July 10, 1941).

These two movies, *Ma, He's Making Eyes at Me* and *Time Out for Rhythm* indicated that Hartmann returned to his roots when he, as a young collegian in the early part of the '30s single-handedly gave birth to the musical *Princess Nita*.

A university tour de force with *Princess Nita* marked the launching of Hartmann's career. (From the collection of Ed Hartmann)

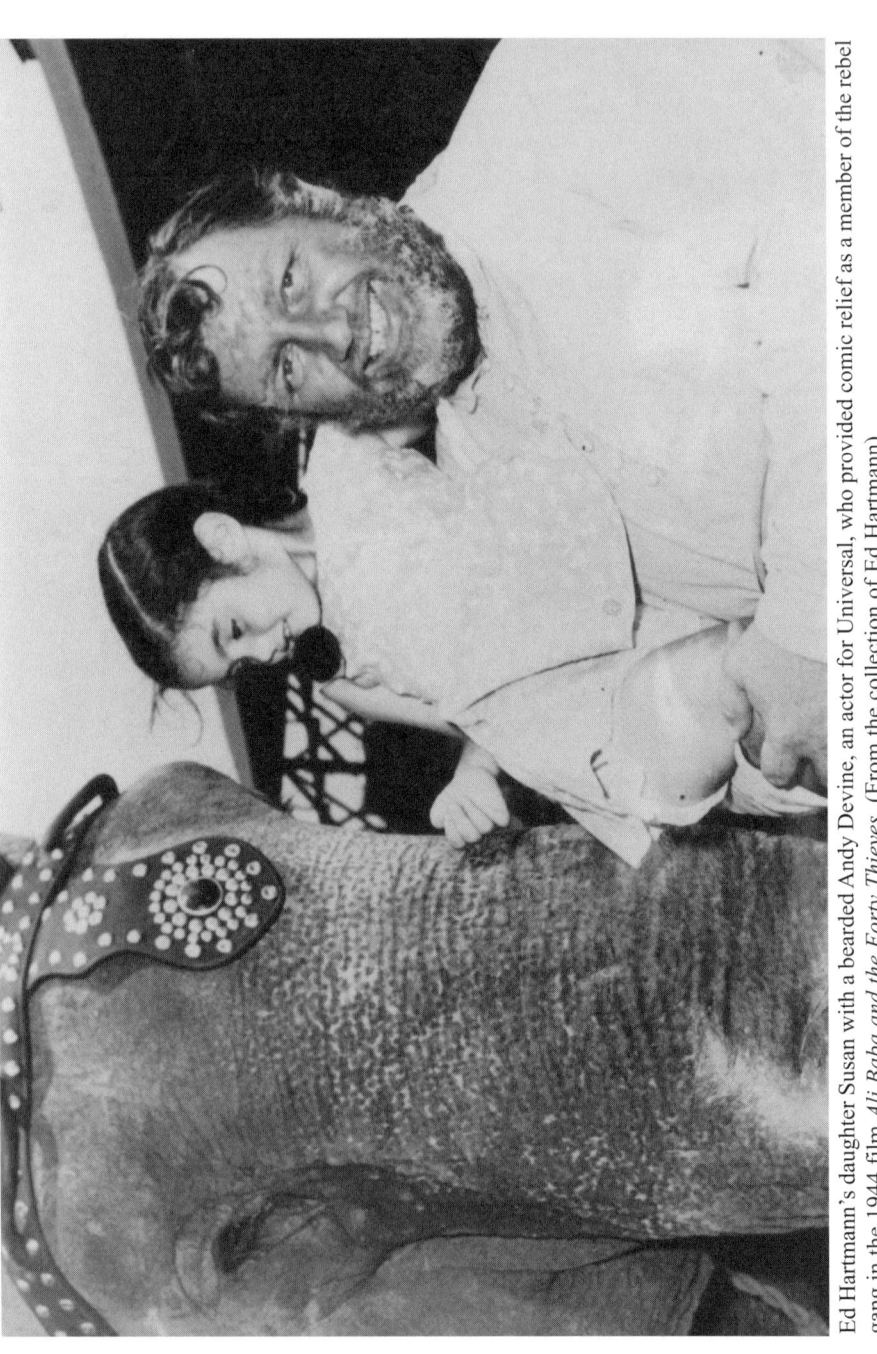

Ed Hartmann's daughter Susan with a bearded Andy Devine, an actor for Universal, who provided comic relief as a member of the rebel gang in the 1944 film *Ali Baba and the Forty Thieves*. (From the collection of Ed Hartmann)

A grown-up Susan on the set of *Casanova's Big Night* (1954), one of seven films Hartmann wrote for Bob Hope. (From the collection of Ed Hartmann)

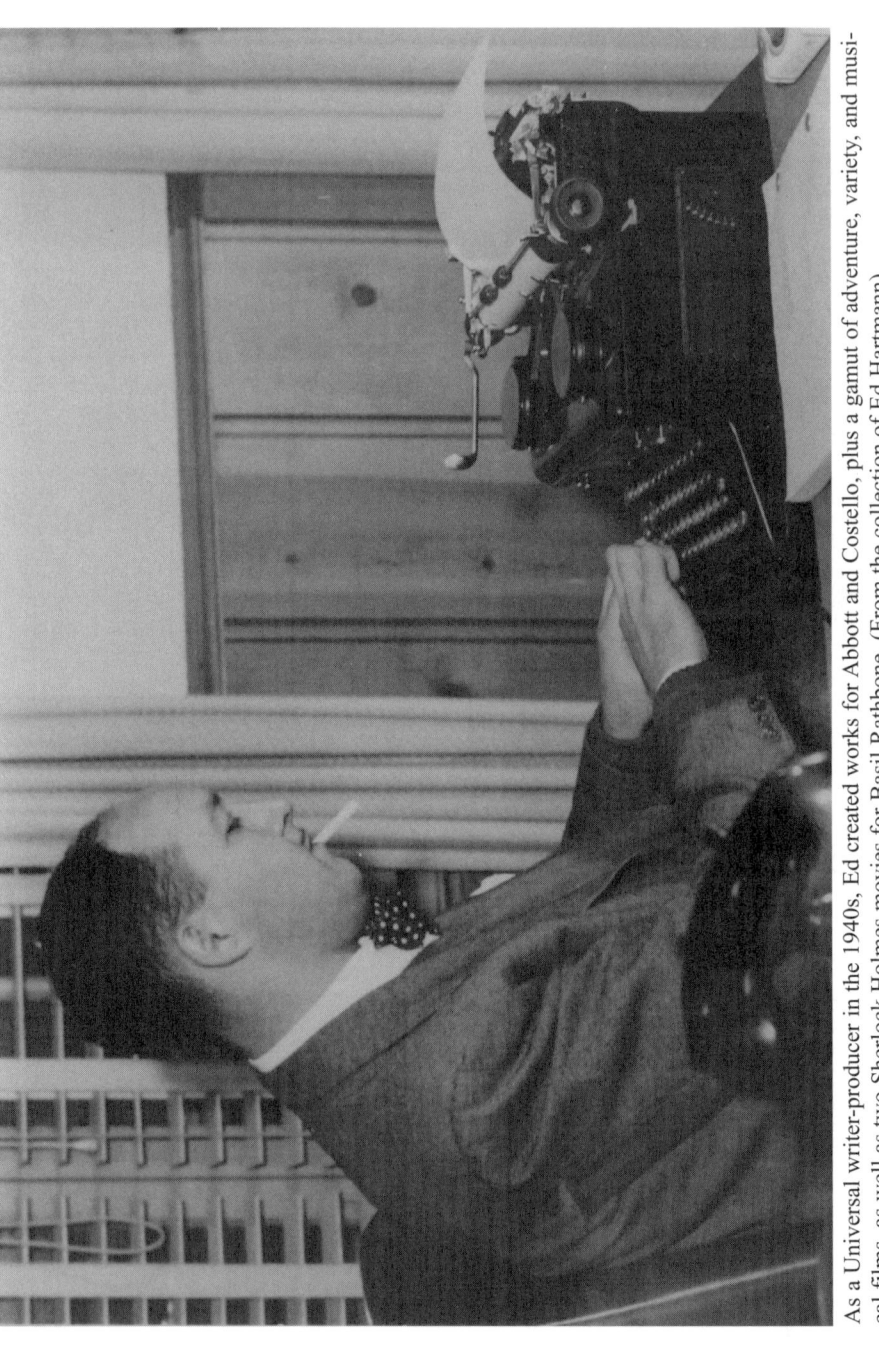

As a Universal writer-producer in the 1940s, Ed created works for Abbott and Costello, plus a gamut of adventure, variety, and musical films, as well as two Sherlock Holmes movies for Basil Rathbone. (From the collection of Ed Hartmann)

A publicity photo of Olson, Hartmann, and Johnson. (From the collection of Ed Hartmann)

Ed created a story for *Here Comes the Co-eds* (1945). Bud and Lou with Martha O'Driscol. (From the collection of Donald McCaffrey)

Producer-writer Hartmann in front of the 1936 *Show Boat* set that he used for the Abbott and Costello vehicle *Naughty Nineties* (1945). (From the collection of Ed Hartmann)

Bud and Lou execute their "Who's on First" vaudeville routine in *Naughty Nineties*, the only feature film in which the duo performed the famous skit. (From the collection of Donald McCaffrey)

3
Creative Independence at Universal

While Edmund found his years with Paramount as his most satisfying period in the Hollywood experience, his Universal years gave him greater independence. When he moved to television he would have even more artistic freedom as producer and writer. However, in the mid-forties Hartmann received authority to handle two comedy teams: Abbott and Costello, and Olsen and Johnson. Ed's independence reigned best when he was both producer and writer in 1944 and 1945.

This first emergence of Hartmann's refined, high-level, humorous writing skills in the '40s didn't materialize until he sold a story to MGM. His original title for his work, *The Gentle Touch*, like a number of his titles, got changed by the powers that be. This one was revised into *The Feminine Touch* (1941). When I happened to catch a broadcast of this film on Turner Classic Movies, I told Ed how much I found this sophisticated comedy as one of the best of the genre. Since he was friend of Preston Sturges, he beamed when I compared his writing to that of a man he admired so much. "My credit lists me as a creator of the story, but I did come in and do some rewriting," Ed explained.

MGM provided humorist writers Ogden Nash and George Oppenheimer as colleagues in the creation of *The Feminine Touch*, and one of its outstanding directors, W. S. Van Dyke, noted for his handling of *The Thin Man* (1934) plus two other films in that popular series of the sophisticated, comic detective genre. The studio also provided four gifted leading actors: Rosalind Russell, Don Ameche, Kay Francis, and Van Heflin. Hartmann's battle of the sexes basic story has elements of the Restoration and eighteenth-century stage drama. The feeling of neglect emerges when a wife feels she is ignored by her husband when other men give her unusual attention. The husband, a college professor enacted by Don Ameche, tries to follow the thesis of his book that disparages men and women for yielding to the emotion of jealousy. His wife, played by Rosalind Russell, becomes indignant and jealous when she thinks he is flirting with other women. Actor Van Heflin portrays a would-be seducer and actress

Kay Francis handles the woman caught in between who ends up with masher Heflin. A number of intrigues develop from the interaction of the two couples that has much of the flavor of a stage drama from the age of the sophisticated court comedy of Shakespeare's *Love's Labour's Lost*.

There might have been a career movement to MGM if political favoritism from producer Arthur Freed had not materialized in the form of an assignment with coscreenwriter Gertrude Purcell to create a script for *Babes on Broadway* (1941), starring the very popular teenage stars, Mickey Rooney and Judy Garland. Hartmann must have yearned to join other contract writers for MGM because the studio was noted for insisting on a quality motion picture—even to the point of not releasing a finished work because it did not reach the standards the company demanded. Movie evaluator Robert Nott reported Ed's reaction to a dark turn of this assignment:

> "The phone rang. It was my agent. He said, 'MGM is letting you go. You're entitled to a week's notice, so you have another week to work, then you're through.' I said, 'That's impossible. I just left the producer who was excited about the first sequence.' My agent said, 'I can't help that. The studio told me that you're through.' So I called Gertrude Purcell and told her. She said, 'They can't do that to you. I'm going to tell them if they fire you, they have to fire me too.' The next morning I was ready to go to the studio and I got a phone call from Gertrude. She said, 'Well, they just fired me!' And she didn't get a week's notice. It turns out that Freed had a guy named Freddy Finklehoffe, who was a personal friend of his whom he'd used on a lot of pictures, and who was evidently working on something else which had fallen through. So Finklehoffe was now available. Freed fired us and brought him in. Typical Hollywood." ("The Kinks of Comedy; Beyond the Laughter with Veteran Screenwriter Ed Hartmann," *Filmfax*, p. 74.)

There may have been many fortuitous events and many political mishaps and maneuvers that propelled Ed to become a regular with Universal. He would make his mark with the company writing the musical comedy and the adventure pictures. Universal would thrive on the comedy with a contemporary setting and the exotic adventure work set in the mid-East of the past. It would help pull the company from bankruptcy.

While it was not clear how Hartmann got linked with the exotic, romantic swashbuckler, however, his first effort in the genre proved to be *Arabian Nights* (1942).

"There was a precursor to your 1943 *Ala Baba and the Forty Thieves*?" I asked by phone, not mentioning the film to get his confirmation on my discovery. Ed replied, "I wrote on the set for *Arabian Nights*, however not enough to get a credit."

I had given Hartmann a videotape of a 1943 film called *Hi, Diddle Diddle*, a weak attempt at sophisticated comedy that someone thought Ed helped write.

"That's completely a Fred Jackson script. I had nothing to do with it."

In an earlier interview Ed told me he didn't like Jackson's scripting.

"I get credit for pictures I didn't write and don't get credit for ones I have written."

"I'm beginning to discover that," I said. "And now I know some scholar for the *American Film Institute Catalogue* got it right for a change with *Arabian Nights.*"

This swashbuckler proved how popular the genre became in the 1940s. Jon Hall and Maria Montez costarred in a half dozen similar films. Often cast with them, Turhan Bey found his career fizzling when the genre ran its course and no longer intrigued audiences.

Arabian Nights employs the plot of rival brothers, enacted by Jon Hall and Leif Erickson, who not only fight for the position of a leader of a kingdom, but also compete for the affection of a dancer named Scheherazade, played by Maria Montez. There exists the usual intrigue of a plotting villain, swordplay clashes on horseback, and the eventual embrace of the hero and heroine, Hall and Montez, of course. More humor is employed in this work than the usual spectacle. There are three comedians: Billy Gilbert as Ahmad, Shemp Howard as Sinbad, and John Qualen as Aladdin. The number of comedy scenes developed in this swashbuckler exceeds those of most of the Universal films of this genre.

Portly Billy Gilbert handled the main comic role as a leader of a traveling troupe of entertainers, acrobats, dancers, and singers. When troubles meet the group Gilbert goes into comic exasperation, wheezing and sneezing. Shemp Howard wants to relate some of his adventures, which Sinbad had many, only to receive bored rejection by his fellow members of the troupe; and John Qualen has the famous lamp that he vainly keeps rubbing to produce a genie. Much to his consternation, the genie never materializes. In *Ali Baba and the Forty Thieves*, only one comedian, Andy Devine, is employed.

As the solo writer for *Ali Baba,* Hartmann had to avoid the standard plot of the story because a British film company was using it. With innovation he recalled the invasion of Mongols who captured and ruled Bagdad. Consequently, the author develops a clash between cultures. The conquering Mongolian leader, Hulaga Khan, not only proved to be an oppressor of the population, he has eyes for the beautiful Amara, enacted by Maria Montez. Hartmann developed intrigue by having Amara's father cooperating with Khan to obtain a high position in the tyrant's regime. And, of course, a rightful heir to the throne of the conquered country emerges in Ali Baba, who has become the leader of the forty thieves. Almost all adventure films of this genre end with a pleasing denouement. Jon Hall as Ali Baba leads his crew of forty, with the help of others, to vanquish the despot and his hoard. Furthermore, the hero, Ali Baba, gets the love of the heroine, Amara.

And the comic relief? Andy Devine gets to care for the boy Ali Baba who seeks refuge with the band of forty men. Partly under the influence of the boy who grows into manhood, the band is metamorphosed from thieves into champions of oppressed people. Devine, as Abdullah—somewhat like a complaining Falstaff, achieves comedy by not liking his role as if he were a woman caring for a child. Abdullah often helps the adult Ali Baba even in times of great danger. At one time he complains about his role: "Still the nursemaid!" Andy actually takes over the role of a sidekick, just like the part he played in a number of

Westerns. Hartmann even gives him the act of dispatching one of the villains of the movie. Earlier in the development of the plot this comic character revealed his Falstaff bluster when he challenged a newcomer to the band. But a duel did not materialize when he realized his opponent had a very sharp knife.

An adventure of this genre needed an actor who could portray Khan as the quintessence of all villains. Kurt Katch, a famous theatre actor in Germany, fled the reign of Hitler because he was a Jew. Ironically he became one of the leading portrayers of demonic Nazi officers in Hollywood. His role of the smirking, lusty Kahn proved to be his best.

Handling his original story Ed received one of his best screen credits. After the main cast listings this designation appeared: "Written for the screen by Edmund L. Hartmann."

Since the success of the exotic swashbuckler would continue, Hartmann would create another one in 1945 for Universal, entitled *Sudan*. Using some of the same actors, Maria Montez, Jon Hall, Turhan Bey, and Andy Devine, the location is changed to ancient Egypt. While Jon Hall plays a secondary role with a comic sidekick Devine, he does help queen Maria Montez conquer a villain played by George Zucco. In this romantic adventure Turhan Bey provides the lead who wins the heart of the queen. Edmund felt this work suffered from added scenes director John Rawlins injected into the original script. However, Hartmann received credit as the sole screenwriter. As late as 1965 Universal tried to revive the eastern swashbuckler using Hartmann's basic idea of the invasion of Mongols in *The Sword of Ali Baba*. The screenwriter obtained credit for the story and some sources give him credit for this screenplay. Also, some footage from Ed's 1944 *Ali Baba and the Forty Thieves* gave this picture the quality of a remake of the earlier work. But the quality of this later work is hindered because it lacks the magic that resulted from combining the acting talents of the original cast.

The screenwriter displayed his eclectic skills in the handling of original Sherlock Holmes stories—that is, tales only loosely based on the works by Arthur Conan Doyle. Universal launched its series of the most famous fictional detectives with instructions to the writers that each narrative must be contemporary. "The studio didn't want to invest in period costumes and sets," Ed remarked when he viewed a clip from the 1943 *Sherlock Holmes and the Secret Weapon*. He worked with Edward T. Lowe and W. Scott Darling in the creation of this second picture in the series. Fortunately, they had Basil Rathbone as Holmes, Nigel Bruce as Dr. Watson, and Lionel Atwill as Professor Moriarty. The updated story had the masterful detective trying to prevent World War II German spies from stealing the secret weapon, a bombsight. Holmes has the mental skills to break secret codes before Moriarty, who, of course, is on the side of the Nazis. The complicated plot with the contemporary wartime intrigue fascinated audiences who liked to see the enemy defeated by the resourceful Sherlock Holmes. With several disguises he invaded the world of the villains and with Dr. Watson's help he evaded Moriarty's attempt to kill the detective.

An even more critically successful work, Ed's second Sherlock Holmes picture, *The Scarlet Claw* (1944), once more used Rathbone and Bruce to advantage. Evaluators now rank this work as one of the best using the characters created by Arthur Conan Doyle. *The Scarlet Claw* has a quality that matches the effectiveness of late '30s Sherlock Holmes pictures released by 20th Century-Fox. In his book *The Detective in Film*, William Everson praises *The Scarlet Claw* as "a genuinely eerie chiller with some echoes of *The Hound of the Baskervilles*" (p. 19). This 1939 work, and *The Adventures of Sherlock Holmes*, released the same year, were precursors of twelve modernized works with the detective that helped pull Universal out of bankruptcy.

The Scarlet Claw has many of the mystery elements of *The Hound of the Baskervilles*. Both films possess environments of the dark world of night where a supposedly supernatural being haunts and kills with savage force. The location in Quebec, Canada, helped give a more authentic touch that followed in the world created by Arthur Conan Doyle. And the complications of the mystery plot might have emerged from the mind of this author. Basil Rathbone and Nigel Bruce as the sleuthing partners proved to be at top form in their portraits. The story development also has a type of innovation by a villain not easily identified. Holmes deduced through his uncanny ability to link clues together that the murderer must be a psychotic actor who sought vengeance on people he imagines wronged him. Sherlock developed the right premise; however, since the actor proved to be a master of disguise he became almost impossible to catch.

The Scarlet Claw, although contemporary critics gave it little notice, now remains the best picture in the series of twelve features released by Universal from 1942 to 1946. Here was another example that Hartmann could handle complicated plots of the mystery as well as the adventure drama—genres that helped him to maintain his status as a writer when he moved to Hollywood in the '30s. Furthermore, he would continue as a writer of mystery stories for the television series *The Thin Man* that ran from September 1957 to June 1959. NBC would offer daytime reruns of the series into the 1960s. Hartmann also tried to produce as well as write another series for CBS in this same period. While *The Thin Man* series was based on the detective stories by Dashiell Hammett, the proposed *Cool and Lam* series was based on Erle Stanley Gardner mystery novels. Gardner voiced his approval of such a series by saying, "The Cool and Lam books have been successful for many years. I hope their TV series will be equally long-lived and successful." But as so many projects in Hollywood and for the networks, the potential project did not materialize.

4
Don't Let the Fat Lady Sing: The Writers

Les White saw the hooded, black figure of death approaching. A gag and screenwriter of such movies as Eddie Cantor's *If You Knew Susie* (1948), Les might have been searching for a line to please others—a bit of dark humor—like Yogi Berra's "It ain't over until it's over." But his bedside companions got a better one as the word "opera" popped into his mind when a fat nurse entered the room. Les, with pretended anguish, said, "Don't sing! Don't sing!"

Another colorful writer, a gag specialist for motion picture cartoons, Frank Tashlin, helped Hartmann create a Bob Hope and Jane Russell vehicle, *The Paleface* (1948), one of the big box office hits of the year. Frank joined a cult where Jane's mother preached with religious fervor that the end of the world was very near. Ed Hartmann learned that Frank shared some of mother Russell's eccentricities. When Tashlin had some problem he announced to Ed that he would have to consult with "the man upstairs." Ed thought he meant the head of the studio. Finally, it became clear that his coauthor wanted to get directions from God.

Furthermore, Hartmann, who loved the thrill of gambling, wanted to go to the racetrack not long after he heard about the predicted Armageddon from Miss Russell's mother. As Ed walked out the door, a deluge hit with wind, rolling clouds, and rain that could have launched the Ark in biblical times. It was temporary chaos, but Ed reported that for one of the few times in history, the race was canceled and he wondered if Jane's mother didn't have some intimate relationship with "the man upstairs."

Gagman Frank from Warner Brothers's Porky Pig cartoons evidently had skills in his profession that would compensate for his unusual views of the supernatural. Besides his ability to create jokes, he was able to convince executives that he could be a director. He went on to direct a sequel to Hope's 1948 hit, *Son of Paleface* (1952) and a number of Jerry Lewis and Dean Martin films, plus Danny Kaye's *The Man from the Diner's Club* (1963). Tashlin also worked on scripts for Red Skelton in the '40s and '50s when the comedian was a rival of such comics as Jerry Lewis. Frank announced to Hartmann that only five great directors existed in Hollywood. "And, of course," Ed said with a wry smile, "Frank said he was one of them." Obviously, this writer-director was full of contradiction. He was shy socially with wacky opinions, but held a high opinion of his professional rank. To Edmund these contradictions proved disconcerting. However, it probably was hard to argue with a man who was almost physically a cartoon character of his early years at the Warner Brothers cartoon factory: a man 6 feet 8 inches tall with a weight of 280 pounds.

One other quirk exhibited by Frank Tashlin made Hartmann wonder if this colleague wanted anyone to come to his house. He would invite someone to his home for dinner. When the guests arrived at the door, Tashlin would instruct his wife and daughter to hide behind a couch. The puzzled visitors would wait and wait some more. Finally they would go away and Frank would signal the "all clear" to his hiding family.

Edmund Hartmann's long, successful career in motion pictures and television was due to his ability to work with a wide variety of writers, directors, and producers. In marked contrast to his relationship with the gag writer Frank Tashlin was Ed's relationship with screenwriters on *The Feminine Touch* (1941). These sophisticated writers were wits with literary backgrounds: George Oppenheimer, a dramatist from the Broadway stage and Ogden Nash, a humorous poet from the *New Yorker* magazine. Hartmann indicated that this motion picture, starring Rosalind Russell, Don Ameche, Kay Francis, and Van Heflin, was a creation he really enjoyed doing. Hartmann invented the story and sold it to MGM before the collaborators assisted in developing this interesting sophisticated comedy that has many characteristics of Restoration and eighteenth-century stage dramas. It is a work using complicated relationships between the sexes with urbane repartee. Earlier works, such as four romantic comedies created in 1938 illustrate how Oppenheimer penned a number of films of the same genre. However, he wrote for the Marx Brothers the year before, *A Day at the Races*.

With similar versatility, Edmund had the ability to work with unruly vaudevillian teams: Abbott and Costello, Olsen and Johnson, and the Ritz Brothers. He also sometimes worked with gagmen who had experience in a variety of stage shows. Such a man was John Grant.

Grant had a working relationship as an actor in vaudeville and in operettas. His mind had catalogued a myriad of routines from his experience, and he developed an ability to put them to work for specific comic groups. He became one of the main scripters for Abbott and Costello. Hartmann produced and wrote two motion pictures, *In Society* (1944) and *Naughty Nineties* (1945), for the popular straightman and comic. Grant assisted him with these films and even earned a producer credit for the latter film. Ed had provided the story for the team's 1941 *Keep 'em Flying*, and John Grant was one of the writers for this film. He would go on to get credit for most of the Bud Abbott and Lou Costello films—a total of about thirty features. Ed observed that Grant's appearance belied his profession for he dressed as though he were a stuffy businessman.

When John Grant wrote for 1955 comedy *Abbott and Costello Meet the Mummy*, he didn't realize it would be the last of a long series of films he would develop for the team. Lou Costello became incensed with Grant's refusal to sight the loyalty oath that was being forced on writers and other Hollywood filmmakers during Senator Joseph McCarthy's investigation of what he thought was an invasion of communists into the creative industry. Comedian Costello broke relations with the writer.

As producer and author for two Abbott and Costello features, Hartmann employed a battery of writers to work for him. Hal Fimberg would work on both *In Society* and *The Naughty Nineties*. He would become a distinguished creator of a spoof of the James Bond spy series with *Our Man Flint* (1966) and *In Like Flint* (1967), using James Colburn as a clever superspy and womanizer.

Two other men, Hugh Wedlock and Howard Snyder, worked on the story for the Abbott and Costello 1944 movie *In Society*. Both writers would also make contributions to other films by this comedy team.

Using a story devised by Eddie Cline, a director of such luminaries as Buster Keaton and W. C. Fields, Hartmann fashioned a script to fit Ole Olsen and Chic Johnson, a team noted for its wacky antics in burlesque and vaudeville. For *Ghost Catchers* Hartmann had a solo screenwriting credit. He also served as producer for this 1944 work and *See My Lawyer* (1945). Cline also directed this Olson and Johnson vehicle, making a contribution to the screenplay.

Hartmann wrote the script for the wackiest team from vaudeville, the Ritz Brothers. While they were not as critically acclaimed as the Marx Brothers were, they did have their following. Ed wrote only one film for them, the 1943 *Hi 'ya, Chum*. This work featured the comic trio's songs, dances, and comic routines sprinkled throughout the picture. Bosley Crowther gives a cynical description of the team's wild antics, "[They] open a restaurant there, they climb all over a kitchen, dress up like cowboys and do an act, cross their eyes, muss their hair— in fact, do everything but reach out from the screen and slap you on the back" (*New York Times*, February 26, 1943, p. 17). It should be realized that there are many fans, who as youths, remember fondly the TV shows of the Three Stooges. And there are fans who remember the Ritz Brothers. Actually, the slapstick trio the Three Stooges would often trade body blows and eye poking with no motivated reason. Their routines were crude compared with those of the Ritz Brothers. The song and dance of the brothers plus their routines had a much better spirit of play and joy, however oddball the brothers' off-the-wall behavior.

The Three Stooges did appear in one musical authored by Hartmann, *Time Out for Rhythm* (1941). The team was, however, only a part of a musical variety show with Ann Miller, Rudy Vallee, and Rosemary Lane.

In another musical, *Variety Girl* (1947), Hartmann worked with a pioneer from the silent age, Monte Brice. He scripted such classics as Raymond Griffith's *Hands Up* and Bebe Daniels's *Miss Brewster's Millions* in 1926. After directing Wallace Berry in *Casey at the Bat* (1927), he returned to screenwriting for other silent screen features. Brice was able to make a transition to the sound motion pictures and by the late '30s contributed his writing talents to variety shows and musicals. Before he was a coauthor with Edmund for *Variety Girl*, he helped with the creation of such lavish musicals as the 1941 *Pot o' Gold* and the 1944 *The Fleet's In.*

In the preface to his book, *The Parade's Gone By* (1968), historian Kevin Brownlow relates how Monte Brice tells how he complained about the way a studio was depicting the shooting of silent pictures. It was for a biography of one of the kings of medium's early years, *The Buster Keaton Story* (1957). An assistant on the set became annoyed with his remarks and cruelly told him to leave: "'Times have changed. You're an old man. The parade's gone by. . . .'" Brownlow found in this remark the title for a study of cinema of the silent age.

One of the most fruitful writer collaborations for Hartmann developed when he wrote scripts with Hal Kanter. Three joint efforts in the early '50s provided vehicles for Bob Hope: *My Favorite Spy, Here Come the Girls,* and *Casanova's Big Night.* All three works are comedies of high quality and there might have been a fourth collaboration. Kanter, Hartmann, and Danny Arnold were assigned a Martin and Lewis 1953 film, *The Caddy.* In his colorful autobiography, *So Far, So Funny,* Kanter stated that although he was learning the art of screenwriting from Ed, he recoiled from the project because Arnold proved to be a novice writer and, most important of all, a Jerry Lewis sycophant. Danny convinced the comedian that he was looking after the star's interest by snitching on the so-called inferior work of Hal and Ed (pp. 187-188). The next year, 1954, Hal returned to work with Ed on *Casanova's Big Night.*

Starting his career as an actor and stand-up comedian, the bootlicker Danny Arnold who offended Kanter so much didn't prosper in feature films as a screenwriter when he left the Lewis and Martin team. However, when he moved to television, he produced and wrote some effective situation comedies, *Barney Miller, That Girl,* and *Bewitched.* Eventually Arnold would get his comeuppance when he could not get his way with TV studio executives. Hartmann's collaborator, Hal Kanter, would provide more important feature screenplays than those penned by Arnold. He executed an effective screen adaptation of the Tennessee Williams play, *The Rose Tattoo* in 1955 and cowrote Frank Capra's last directing project, *Pocketful of Miracles* (1961). Kanter also was successful in the media of radio and television. Hal scripted radio programs for such celebrities as Danny Kaye, Bing Crosby, and Jack Parr. Kanter moved to television in the medium's formative years, developing a comedy show for Ed Wynn in 1948. He later wrote for Lucille Ball and was an executive producer of *All in the Family* in the '70s, one of the most popular TV series of the decade.

Since Ed became a prominent screenwriter, producer, and head of the Writers Guild, I wanted to know the status of authors of film scripts in the decades that Edmund Hartmann plied his talents. We talked about the art of storytelling in a golden age of popular literature. The decades of the '30s through the '50s witnessed many short stories in almost any magazine. It was the age when some of our most significant novelists emerged in the United States: Ernest Hemingway, F. Scott Fitzgerald, William Faulkner, and John Steinbeck. All of these literary giants had some brush with Hollywood and many of their works were adapted to the screen. For each one of these famous authors there were three decades with many minor writers who had skills that included well-developed plots and characters. Dramatic writers for the stage Lillian Hellman, Tennessee Williams, Arthur Miller, and William Inge were also model authors who witnessed adaptations of their works. They developed a new movement in the theatre in the '40s and '50s. Eugene O'Neill wrote plays two decades earlier but produced some great works in the '50s.

Ed and I agreed on the importance of these writers and wondered whether some newer literary movement could provide good examples for screenwriters of today. And, of course, I wondered why the talent of film writers didn't receive more recognition in the years from the '30s to the '50s.

A trace of bitterness came to Hartmann's voice when he told me how the studio executives treated contract writers. They viewed directors as the most important part in the creation of the movie.

"To change directors in the middle of a production disrupted the system. Much easier to hire another writer."

"Writers were expendable," I remarked, not realizing it was obvious.

We discussed the role of the writer as the progenitor and the essence of the creation. We agreed that much of the problems of many movies today resulted from faulty or ineffective scripts.

"As an evaluator of dramatic films I sometimes detect another critic stealing some of my ideas. What did you feel when you were withdrawn from a production? Then, along comes a writer and takes all the credit for your efforts. I bet you developed thick skin."

He frowned, "I never did."

We continued with an exploration of what it felt like to be fired from a studio after effective scripts were produced and forced to seek work for another studio.

Ed explained that it often resulted from an executive in a political situation and the flock of writers looking for a job. Hartmann was a survivor brimming with original stories and could make the transition.

With some of his dry wit he observed, "You get no sympathy from colleagues when you're fired. They would hope you'd get run over by a truck so they could get your position."

Persistence and talent carried Ed on. It was never over for him because the fat lady didn't get a chance to sing.

5
Send in the Clowns

Lou Costello with spontaneous, obsessive desire reproduced an elaborate routine used by Harold Lloyd, a famous silent comedian who had moved to sound films.

"It was already in the can," Ed explained as the producer of the Abbott and Costello vehicle, *In Society* (1944). Lou pushed the production forward with a gag-by-gag repetition of the magician's coat sequence from the 1932 *Movie Crazy*. Lou's version had been shot and was ready to be added to the picture. Hartmann knew the chubby comedian was naïve enough to not realize Lloyd might sue Universal for use of his copyrighted film. This routine featured the hapless Harold dancing with the studio boss's wife—a dowager with the essence of propriety. Since the would-be Hollywood actor in the plot of *Movie Crazy* had mistakenly donned a magician's tuxedo coat instead of his own, a deluge of tricks fell from hidden pockets: eggs, scarves, live chicks, and even a live rabbit. Comedy develops through the frustrated young man's attempt to hide the items that drop from the coat. This routine would fit more aptly the embarrassment comedy that became comedian Lloyd's forte. Even if the studio did not receive a hefty lawsuit for copying this routine, it was a type of comedy that would not fit the character Costello portrayed. This sequence from *Movie Crazy* focused on Lloyd's humor of social embarrassment and the comedy of frustration as he attempted to hide the fact that he had anything to do with the objects that appeared. Lou's standard comedy character proved to be too naïve to handle this type of genteel material.

I indicated to Edmund that the dumping of this magician coat routine from *In Society* could have been a prudent idea. I interviewed Harold Lloyd in the late '60s and he was disturbed when some comedy writers or directors moved from his studio to another and tried to reproduce total sequences that he helped invent in some of his films.

While Hartmann wrote either the story or screenplay for five of Abbott and Costello's films, he only had the added control of producing two of them, *In Society* (1944) and *The Naughty Nineties* (1945). He met a number of problems with this added responsibility. Ed found the duo capricious in the handling of his scripts. "They wanted to add old routines from their days in burlesque. Sometimes the skits worked," the screenwriter-producer indicated. While some critics, such as Bosley Crowther (in his review of *The Naughty Nineties, New York Times*, June 21, 1945, p. 18) thought the chestnut "Who's on First" proved to be too hoary with age, fans of the two comedians find such a routine delightful.

Hartmann explained the irony of the success of Abbott and Costello. "They thought their career in films was over and had packed their bags to go back to New York and the stage." However, Universal realized that the team's 1941 *Buck Privates* had gained a wide audience and the comedians were stopped from leaving and given a contract with more money. Ed got into the story and screenwriting of another service-related comedy for the duo, as well as a comic thriller and a Western. The same year of the army comedy's hit, 1941, Hartmann worked on *Keep 'em Flying* and *Hold That Ghost*. A year later he developed a story for *Ride 'em Cowboy,*

It would appear director Arthur Lubin restrained the duo from inserting a number of their routines from the stage in the production of *Keep 'em Flying*. Several skits with comedienne Martha Raye smack of a vaudeville origin. The talented Ms. Raye enacts a dual role as twin sisters (Barbara Phelps and Gloria Phelps), which creates consternation for the naïve Lou Costello, playing the role of an airplane mechanic with the name of Heathcliff. Entering the World War II recreation center for military inductees, the USO, the two comedians attempt to order food at a restaurant counter. The twins work in the kitchen and Heathcliff has difficulty ordering when he thinks the twin Barbara is the same woman from whom he requested food. This twin, Gloria, is the comic girlfriend of Heathcliff, with the woman becoming the aggressor in a number of skits.

Keep 'em Flying has a number of broad slapstick scenes and sequences. Early in the movie Abbott as Blackie Benson proves to be the con man who tries to force his chubby friend to act as the umpire in a carnival booth called "Hit the Umpire." Heathcliff realizes that people will throw baseballs that would bounce off his head and he refuses. As Blackie pushes him into a position behind a dummy baseball player who is in front of the umpire, the mechanical dummy swings the bat and knocks the protesting Heathcliff repeatedly as the victim tries to escape going back and forth. It becomes a typical routine of the comedy pair showing the con man pushing his friend into a knockabout slapstick scene. With appropriate overstatement Lou Costello sways, knees buckling, to achieve comedy. This scene works, but Lou executes a number of pratfalls throughout the picture that become gratuitous. By far the broadest slapstick humor develops when the comedians Abbott and Costello accidentally start an airplane and take off with no knowledge of how to maneuver it. Fall guy Lou ends up sliding around on the wing of the plane and hanging on with comic desperation. Much of this routine becomes hackneyed even though Costello shows adroit physical movements standing up, falling down, and stuck headfirst in the cockpit.

Keep 'em Flying possesses many features of a musical. Leads Carol Bruce and Dick Foran, at different times in the film, sing with a male chorus what is intended as a title song: "Let's Keep 'em Flying." Bruce gets to handle the climactic production number of this song with many planes flying above her. Multitalented Martha Raye contributes a jazzy song and dance, "Pig Foot Pete." Ms. Bruce, providing the romantic interest with Mr. Foran, has the most songs in the picture. For example, she sings "I'm Looking for the Boy with the Wistful Eyes" as she and Foran take a boat through the tunnel of love. While *Keep 'em Flying* cannot be classified as a full-fledged musical, it becomes a pattern for "a comedy with music" that is often used in an Abbott and Costello movie. Bud Abbott doesn't get engaged in the musical numbers, but Lou occasionally gets into a comic dance, such as his oddball dance with comedienne Joan Davis in *Hold That Ghost* (1941).

While Hartmann did not receive recognition for some writing for *Hold That Ghost*, he did get a credit for the story of the 1942 *Ride 'em Cowboy*. Universal had run the gamut of service comedies for Abbott and Costello: the United States Army, Navy, and Air Force. So, a turn to a variety of civilian professions and different locations became necessary to provide some variety in the comedy of the famous team. In a last gasp for variety and to give Lou the opportunity to display comic fear, the studio hit on the idea of using the medium for self-reflective "meeting" pictures, which were burlesques of such earlier Universal pictures as *Frankenstein, Dr. Jekyll and Mr. Hyde, The Invisible Man,* and *The Mummy*.

Hartmann, who proved to be most successful with his comic Western *Paleface* in 1948, had his first effort in this genre with *Ride 'em Cowboy*. While the picture could have been released a year earlier, *Keep 'em Flying* appeared before to take advantage of the two other 1941 military comedies, *Buck Privates* and *In the Navy*. In this comedy Western, Abbott and Costello play rodeo vendors who tag along, once more, with lead Dick Foran as the hero and romantic interest, who here tries to prove his mettle as a cowboy who was born in the East. Foran ends up getting the girl and winning in a rodeo. The comic pair get in trouble with Indians because Lou accidentally becomes betrothed to an obese woman of the tribe. Musical elements become an important part of *Ride 'em Cowboy*. One of the great soloist of the time, Ella Fitzgerald, sings "I'll Remember April" and she introduced a song she developed with Al Friedman, "A Tisket, A Tasket"— a novelty song that became a big hit. Vocal groups the Hi-Hatters, the Jivin' Jacks and Jills, and the Merry Macs fill the picture with many tunes and Foran also shows his skill as he did in *Keep 'em Flying* with a singing voice that is better than his acting talent. With such a contribution of musical groups and soloists it would seem *Ride 'em Cowboy* became a musical. However, the comedy with music almost seemed to be to a subgenre that became Edmund L. Hartmann's forte.

Universal evidently recognized Ed's skill with what surely is a sub-genre staple of the World War II movie industry. They awarded him the producer-writer position for the 1944 *In Society* and the 1945 *The Naughty Nineties*. These were very popular vehicles for Abbott and Costello. As if this were not enough for the prolific screenwriter to handle, he was given the task of handling, the same two years, the total creation of two works for vaudevillians Ole Olsen and Chic Johnson, *Ghost Catchers* (1944) and *See My Lawyer* (1945).

In Society employed a comic destruction action by the leading humorous characters that often became the quintessence of a routine used by the Three Stooges or Laurel and Hardy. Incompetent professionals wreak havoc. Abbott and Costello as plumbers Eddie and Albert attempt to fix a leak in a bathroom and turn a dribble into a waterfall. Comedy is achieved by showing incompetent professionals trying their best to ply their trade. Much like the Hardy of another duo, Abbott elects himself as the boss. He browbeats his partner for false attempts to fix the minor leak in a washbasin. Progressively the dribble increases and springs forth in the showerhead. Lou as Albert pounds on the wall and breaks the pipe over the bathtub. Now the water gushes to the point it cannot be stopped. In their consternation the pair forget there is a cutoff valve and the bathroom and an adjoining bedroom are flooded. The climax of the scene shows the plumbers in the bathtub floating out a door with Lou yelling, "Head for the hills!"

The damage caused by bungling plumbers is so severe to the house of the Van Cleves that a letter is sent to Eddie and Al. By mistake they receive the wrong letter, inviting them to a weekend on the estate of the Winthropes. Since the plumbers are out of their class, this pair make many faux pas because they are not a part of the rich crowd.

Before they travel to attend the weekend party the comic team employ an ancient vaudeville routine, originally a search for Floogel Street to deliver some hats. The name of the street got changed to Bagel Street—maybe because the sound of the original has a kind of burlesque double meaning, possibly sexual. The basic routine, however, seems intact with possible additions, as Al is given the job of delivering a large sack of straw hats. When a passing stranger is asked the location of Bagel Street and that Al says he will deliver hats to the Susquehanna Hat Company the man becomes so angry he pulls off one of the hats that Al has put on his head and tears it apart. Eddie tells Al he must pay for the hat that was ruined. While Al objects, he pulls another hat from the sack and wears it. A passing woman is asked the location of the street. She starts screaming that her husband was killed on Bagel Street. In a rage she tears the second hat apart. A similar confrontation develops with another woman who screams that she hates the name. The fourth person to attack one of the hats on Al's head claims he is not alive. He declares he was minding his own business on Bagel Street "when a safe fell fifteen stories on my head and killed me." A policeman intervenes when he sees the altercation. The officer starts to take this madman away. The man objects, "I'm dead. You can't arrest me, I'm dead."

This strange skit from the past seems to be as disjointed and crazy as the insane man. In a 1986 interview for a Canadian broadcasting program, Hartmann explained this routine, "I did some research on it and found out it originally made sense. The idea of "Floogel Street" is the man is hired to deliver some hats. And everyone he meets and asks where is Floogel Street, and they beat him up and break up his hats." Ed went on to indicate the original intent was tied to a strike at a hat company. The deliveryman became a strikebreaker. Ed said, "As the comics went on they dropped that and anything that didn't get a laugh. It became lunacy."

The climactic sequence of *In Society* has Eddie and Al chasing the thieves who stole a priceless painting from the Winthrope mansion. Without much logic the pair run to a firehouse and hop a fire truck to pursue the robbers. The sequence utilizes footage from a 1941 Universal W. C. Fields picture *Never Give a Sucker an Even Break*. In this work, Fields races his car to get a woman to a hospital because he thinks she is about ready to deliver a baby. To his disgust, a fire engine gets in his way and a long ladder on the truck with two hooks punctures the roof of his car and the vehicle is lifted up in the air. With inserted shots of Al on the ladder, there is a match with longer shots used in the Fields movie. Al climbs down from his ladder and fights the crooks until the car slips loose and crashes. Al climbs from the wreck with the painting. As he presents the valuable work of art to Mrs. Winthrop, he accidentally walks into it—ripping the canvas beyond repair. And this is the capping gag for the end of the movie.

To the Canadian interviewer Ed said that he would use a couple of the burlesque routines in the pictures he produced and if he didn't want them to do the skits they would do the scenes anyway. In short, Abbott and Costello were incorrigible. It is a wonder that Hartmann could handle them with enough effectiveness when he produced *In Society* and *The Naughty Nineties*. And, it is a wonder the films turned out to be so effective and among the best of the many Abbott and Costello pictures.

As a biographer and evaluator of Hartmann's motion pictures, I should note that *The Naughty Nineties* remains a favorite of critics of the Abbott and Costello creations. Fans of Abbott and Costello, of course, have different tastes. Often they prefer what might be called a cult work filled with slapstick clichés. *The Naughty Nineties* does contain a deluge of slapstick, mostly executed by Lou Costello, but director Jean Yarbrough seemed to have more finesse in handling this type of comedy. However there are a number of features of the work that have impressed critics: 1) A unity of all production elements, especially the music in the picture; 2) The Abbott and Costello character portrayals are more consistent; 3) The plot remains simple and direct; 4) There is a big picture quality by Universal that an Abbott and Costello movie often lacked.

During the World War II years, variety and comedy presentations by Hollywood studios gave the public entertaining creations that consisted of a jumbled bunch of sketches with loosely constructed and thin plots. One of the major problems was the musical numbers that often were poorly motivated—just pasted in as if this element were a whim of any moment in the plot development. *The Naughty Nineties* has the setting of a river showboat and the music numbers exist in a natural environment. It becomes an element that is not forced and is a natural part of show business. Of course, some musicals are focused on stage productions in the process of rehearsal and a final public showing. Some of the pictures of this genre are unified works, such as the 1933 *Footlight Parade*, starring James Cagney, Ruby Keeler, and Dick Powell. However, so many of the variety shows of the '40s don't have this quality, and full-fledged musicals seldom appeared in this decade, at least at Universal. Most of the comedies added musical elements using a strong comedy plot. In the opening sequence of *The Naughty Nineties,* a band and a solo "On a Sunday Afternoon" are presented to the public to advertise the evening entertainment on the showboat. Lou Costello is shown beating a bass drum as a comic bungler named Sebastian Dinwiddle, and the captain of the showboat introduces Bud Abbott as the leading actor Dexter Broadhurst. While the leading female entertainer of the showboat, actress Lois Collier as Caroline, presents most of the songs, even Lou and Bud sing in this picture. Ms. Collier, as the romantic interest, renders several love songs well integrated into the plot. Lou auditions for Bud his version of "My Bonnie Lies over the Ocean," intending to show his ability to join in an act for the showboat. Bud, in a baseball uniform sings briefly "Take Me out to the Ball Game" just before the famous "Who's on First?" routine. Therefore, most musical elements are not gratuitous—that is, stuck in haphazardly, but coordinated with the plot.

The character development of Bud as Dexter and Lou as Sebastian has a consistency not always present in some of their films. Bud remains a self-assured leading actor and Lou continues in *The Naughty Nineties* as an incompetent, oddball assistant. For example, Bud remains poised as he is introduced before the crowd in the first sequence. He also has composure as he enacts the role of the hero in an old-fashioned melodrama.

On the other hand, Lou as the stagehand in charge of effects intrudes on the action onstage.

Costello provides effective comedy in this early sequence with Abbott as a lead in the showboat presentation of a melodrama. Bud does a credible job of acting, in an exaggerated style, the stilted dialogue of the play. Lou creates sound effects backstage as Bud mentions a train and a horse. Followed by his blowing of a special whistle he makes strange chugging sounds with his mouth and uses halves of two coconut shells to create the sound of a horse approaching. The sounds are superficial insertions when the train and horse are merely mentioned. But Lou's most intrusive presence comes when he wanders on stage. When Bud says, "Go away," Lou pulls on the knob of a door and the set of the play caves in. The bumbling stage assistant then pulls a rope that releases a snowfall in the middle of a room.

Producers-screenwriters Edmund Hartmann and John Grant are helped by gagman Felix Adler who is given opening screen credits for "additional comedy sequences." However, as Ed indicated in an interview, gagmen were ineffective in plot development—the story line had to be crafted by those with that special skill.

The basic plot of *The Naughty Nineties* focuses on the attempt by three con artist gamblers to take over the showboat to use it as a casino. With a weakness for gambling, Captain Sam loses his showboat to the gamblers. At a nightclub called the Gilded Cage, Sam (played by mild-mannered Henry Travers) gets drunk and loses to the gamblers. They claim their interest in the showboat and become oppressive partners. This provides the basic conflict and the motivation for Dexter and Sebastian to attempt a way to return the boat to Captain Sam and his daughter Caroline.

At the Gilded Cage the pair try to keep Sam from gambling and a woman villain, part of the gambler trio, tries to slip naïve Sebastian a drink with knockout drops. Comedy is achieved as Lou and conniving woman Bonita (played by

Rita Johnson) switch the tainted drink a number of times in order to avoid drinking it. Lou finally pretends to consume the "Mickey Finn" and instead throws the drink into a potted plant. The plant wilts. This sequence shows Lou attempting to be clever as he struggles. The comedian uses one of his standard character facets, humorous frustration.

At the Gilded Cage the buddies, Dexter and Sebastian, need to get into the gambling room and get a regular patron, a drunk played by Jack Norton, to vouch for them. This actor, Norton, made his living portraying cameo, comic drunks. In this film he gets the pair in the gambling room and remarks, "You stay here until I see where I left you." In the room with all types of games of chance, Bud and Lou, show their dismay as they lose money on a crooked roulette wheel. When they bet on number 33, the roulette ball goes to that number and mysteriously jumps to number 26. Later the pair try to best the gamblers on the showboat when the villainous trio, Crawford, Bonita, and Bailey, bring corruption to the riverboat.

The highlight routine of *The Naughty Nineties* is the favorite burlesque sketch "Who's on First?" It is a classic example of comic cross talk. The frame of reference lapses into total confusion for the comedian but the straight man knows exactly the use of nicknames. A portion of the routine gives some sense of two people conversing at cross-purposes:

> Bud: You know, strange as it may seem, they give ballplayers peculiar names nowadays. On the St. Louis team, Who's on first. What's on second, and I Don't Know is on third.
> Lou: That's what I want to find out. I want you to tell me the names of the fellows on the St. Louis team.
> Bud: I'm telling you. Who's on first. What's on second. I Don't Know is on third.
> Lou: You know the fellows' names?
> Bud: Yes.
> Lou: I mean the fellow's name on first base.
> Bud: Who.

There is complete confusion as the conversation continues with Lou using the names of What and I Don't Know in his inquiry to find out names of the players that make sense. Giving up the pursuit, Lou is exasperated and will not inquire further. He says, "I don't care." To this Bud says, "Oh, that's the short stop."

In this famous routine that Abbott and Costello would repeat many times in their career, Lou employs one of his main techniques—frustration comedy, using an overstatement of his confusion.

One facet of *The Naughty Nineties* that stands out is the big picture quality. The opening sequence utilized a marching band before a large crowd. There are many sets, especially the depicting of many parts of the showboat. There was a godsend for the production in this respect. Universal had sets left over from the

1936 *Show Boat*. Also, the cast attired in period costumes provides a more opulent air to the movie. This gave the quality of an "A" budgeted film on a more stringent budget.

Edmund Hartmann received credit for an original story for *Here Come the Co-Eds*. As the title indicates, this is a college picture—a staple for many comedies in the '30s and '40s. In this film a sister of Slats McCarthy named Molly gets a scholarship to attend a women's college, and Slats, played by Bud Abbott, and his friend, Oliver, enacted by Lou Costello, become caretakers at this institution, Bixby College. The basic plot revolves around the difficulties of Slats and Oliver as they bungle their job as caretakers just as they proved inefficient as plumbers in *In Society*. The two, however, redeem themselves by helping the college financially when they expose the gamblers who bet on a women's basketball game and, without any moral scruples, take the money from the crooks to help Bixby College.

There are two routines executed by Abbott and Costello that show possible links to burlesque sketches. Lou's attempts to tell a story that proves a great humiliation as he relates a tale of Jonah and the whale. He claims it is a joke he invented. Costello declares, "The only thing is I tell this by myself." knowing Abbott's typical dominance of all their conversations. As Lou sets forth the basic concept: "It's about a whale, a ship, and Jonah." Bud interrogates: "What kind of whale?" plus every aspect of the poor narrator's struggle to impress a class of young women at the college. Lou steams at every question that interrupts his joke. Bud ignores his protests and tells the finish of a hackneyed punch line. Finally the poor little fellow moves slowly away from Bud, thoroughly cowed—in silent, comic despair. It is one of the innovative, pantomime moments Costello displays. It remains one of the best touches in all of his film portraits.

Broader humor develops when Costello consumes oyster soup in the college cafeteria. In a fantastic bit, a "wild" oyster pokes its shell from the middle of the bowl to eat a soda cracker the hapless Lou wants to put in his soup. He tries to fish for the mollusk with his tie and is pulled face down into the bowl.

Even broader comedy moves to slapstick in a sequence used by many comedians as a way to get money. To gain financial support for the college, Lou as Oliver wrestles the masked marvel. Joe E. Brown employs a similar wrestling match in his *The Gladiator* (1938). In both movies brutes outmatch the comic characters; however, by pluck and luck by unusual accidents the comedian wins.

More than many of the Abbott and Costello films, *Here Come the Co-Eds* becomes a picture that comes close to being a musical. The extent of the musical elements and the variety of the numbers give it some of this characteristic. One dance and song bit features Lou with a skilled comedienne, Peggy Ryan. The title of the song has a juvenile sexual allusion, but the results appear to be innocent. Lou and Peggy sing a duet and end up with a comic jitterbug caper. As the women's basketball team confronts the rival girls college athletic team of Carlton College, Peggy performs as the lead singer and dancer for a rousing number, "Jumpin' on Saturday Night." It is a type of half-time entertainment that becomes a production number with many women backing up Peggy's twirling, jumping tap dance. Her ability in this department matches her comic turns with Lou Costello. Her facility for perky, oddball behavior becomes an asset, as did the style of Martha Raye in *Keep 'em Flying* and Joan Davis in *Hold That Ghost*. Peggy's manner is that of a natural actress, with a freshness of spontaneity.

Part of the reason this work comes close to the musical is the wartime novelty of an all-girl orchestra and chorus. Since *Here Come the Co-Eds* existed a decade before television, the group had become popular on radio. The billing of one program touted these women entertainers this way: "Phil Spitalny and His Hour of Charm All Girl Orchestra featuring Evelyn and Her Magic Violin." Since many audience members only heard the performances on radio, they wanted to see the group at the movies.

Ed handled many writing assignments, and, more important, as producer of *The Naughty Nineties* and *In Society*, he observed the eccentricities of the team of Abbott and Costello—especially Lou. "He was a man of great heart and could suddenly turn it off and display an inner rage that was almost always there. When he did a comedy routine we let him go on no matter what he said or what he did. And quite often we would maybe have to cut out the whole thing because what came through was not this very dear little fat man but an enraged man."

A cowriter, John Grant, would continue with Abbott and Costello into the '50s. He was with the team from their burlesque days, reported to have been their main writer and the originator of many of their routines, such as "Who's on First?" However, this is not known for sure since he adapted sketches that were handed down from comedian to comedian in vaudeville and burlesque. Such a work as "Floogel Street" must have received some adaptation by Grant. He was one of the few writers who refused to bend to the wishes of the House Un-American Activities. To naïve Costello he became a traitor and the close relationship that went back to the team's burlesque days was cut off. With the estrangement of Lou and Bud severing the duo, their screen days ended. Ironically, a television cartoon of the pair brought back some shade of the success from the past. Both ended up on poverty row—mostly from their income tax evasions.

Edmund Hartmann obviously could juggle many assignments at the same time. He had Universal's assignment to write one film for the Ritz Brothers and the task of writing and producing two films for the Olsen and Johnson duo.

Under the oddball title of *Hi 'Ya, Chum*, Ed created an original story and screenplay for the trio who had the apt name of the Merry Madcaps for the film. There is little doubt that Hartmann knew he must fashion a screwy script for one of the craziest comic team in this entire flood of 1940 variety shows. One of the examples of the wacky humor of the brothers is revealed in the early part of the film. The scene opens with a ballet showing many young women dancing in tutus. A dolly down the line of the dancers shows close view of the legs of the ballerinas. The spindly legs of two of the Ritz brothers are revealed, engaged in lampoon of classical music. They break from the group of women and dance together with a jitterbug fling of a '40s fad. The third brother as ballet master objects to the departure from the classical mode, but the two in tutus win the argument and he joins in the contemporary jazz dance. Obviously ludicrous, this caper in drag remains as evidence the trio would do anything for a laugh. This sketch is funny and shows that they were comics with flair.

The brothers return to the song and dance routines in the middle and end portion of the film. This second number shows them in cowboy attire singing "Cactus Pete for Sheriff" and the last number show them at their antic best. "You Gotta Have Personality" shows the Ritz Brothers using a banterlike exchange which is typical of some of their best routines. Breaking from the song and dance, they imitated some of the popular stars of the decade. One brother with a French accent of Charles Boyer asks another (playing the woman), "May I kiss your lily-white hand?" The third pulls his straw hat into the shape of a bonnet and executes what seems to be a burlesque interpretation of Katharine Hepburn.

While the Ritz Brothers are not for everyone's taste, the team appeals to the adult while the Three Stooges are favorites for children and those who like the most crude of gratuitous slapstick. Hartmann does motivate most of the shenanigans of the comedians. The basic plot concerns the traveling professional performers whose show, "Fancies of 1945," closes in Joplin. The Merry Madcaps travel toward California when their ancient car breaks down in a old ghost town called Rustler's Gulch that witnessed a resurgence and turned into a boom town. The trio and two women from the failed, itinerant troupe find employment in a restaurant. Eventually, this place turns into a nightclub with added women entertainers. The transformation develops because there is a shortage of women in the town. And, of course, the club provides a place for the Madcaps with Sunny and Madge, a two-woman singers' act from their "Fancies" tour to reapply their profession.

If an evaluator were to compare the Ritz Brothers to any other comedy team it should not be the Three Stooges. Instead a critic might call them a poor man's Marx Brothers. However, that might be an underestimate of their talent. Hartmann's use of group's name for *Hi 'ya Chum* certainly shows his insight. The trio's Merry Madcap label says it all. There is a rollicking, manic humor in their horseplay. At times they engage in rapid-fire cross-purpose exchanges—other times one brother tries to top the other, followed by the third reaching the height of absurdity. Ed Hartmann finds the absurdity carried over to someone in the studio administration who invented the title, *Hi 'ya, Chum*. According to the *American Film Catalog* the working title for the picture was *Passing the Buck*.

Hartmann took over the writing and producing task for two Olsen and Johnson creations, *Ghost Catchers* and *See My Lawyer*. Longtime vaudevillians, Chic Johnson played the comic to Ole Olsen's straight man. They paired off in 1914, and by 1918, as they toured the United States, they became headliners. "When they appeared on the screen it was obvious they were old," Ed observed. "On the stage you didn't notice it, but the camera gave them away." Hartmann, however, found them more cooperative than Abbott and Costello, even though he realized they did not have the drawing power that Bud and Lou had. Nevertheless, he felt the two films he wrote and produced, especially *Ghost Catchers*, were worthy projects.

His first work for Ole and Chic had much of the same "old dark house" comedy motif of *Hold That Ghost.* Ed did some writing for that 1941 film so he had the experience with this subgenre of the humorous movie. In *Ghost Catchers,* released three years later, Olsen and Johnson investigate a New York brownstone that supposedly has a previous owner who returns from the grave to haunt the house. The haunting turns out to be mostly a ruse by crooks who wanted to steal a stash of expensive liquor left over from the turn of the century. Humor is provided by creepy incidents devised by the thieves plus the reactions of fear from the inhabitants of the brownstone. One clever touch by the author and producer, Hartmann, evolved when some unexplained occurrences happened. Without any human hands, a bottle tips to pour a drink in a glass; candlesticks move across a table and up into the air; a young woman (played by Gloria Jean) periodically complains of someone pinching her; a white flag waves. Olsen and Johnson play loud jazz to scare away the ghost. The flag appeared because the deceased owner who hoarded all the liquor only liked classical music. And, it turns out the ghost does exist. When the unseen phenomenon materializes, it turns out to be the tippling playboy of the past, played by the actor almost always cast as a drunk, Jack Norton. This mover of the candlesticks provides an in-joke on the happenings in Abbott and Costello's *Hold That Ghost.* Standing before a candlestick on a table, Olsen and Johnson observe that the 1941 film was a "very unbelievable picture" because of the moving of such objects. As this is uttered the candlestick starts sliding back and forth. Such referential in-jokes were used in their works. In *Hellzapoppin'* Ole and Chic move across an Eskimo landscape and observe a small sled. "Wasn't that burned?" came the line with a reference that would have been unknown to any in the audience who had not seen the 1941 *Citizen Kane.*

Ghost Catchers evolves into one of the best works created by Ed Hartmann. Some critics, of whom I as an evaluator am included, give this picture a four-star rating.

While *Ghost Catchers* employs some of the gags Ole and Johnson brought to the picture, it has the plot elements not found in their "blackout" type of stage shows. When stage director H. C. Potter moved to Hollywood with the long-running Broadway hit, *Hellzapoppin',* Universal assigned writers Nat Perrin and Warren Wilson to give the musical revue some substance, as the establishment viewed the way to improve the wacky work. The studio employed some of their high profile comics, Martha Raye, Mischa Auer, and Hugh Herbert. Also, the writers added a story line of producing a musical and, of course, a romantic triangle of two men striving for the affection of a woman. Hartmann had a similar task in developing a story line for Olsen and Johnson to sprinkle on their outrageous puns and props.

Hartmann felt his creation of *Ghost Catches* proved to be much better than *See My Lawyer,* an adaptation from a stage play. A contemporary review, March 4, 1945, in the *New York Times* indicated the film was not one of the best shows of that decade:

> Those zany, slap-stickers, Olsen and Johnson, are back at the same old pie-slinging, seltzer-squirting routines in *See My Lawyer.*

The plot, like the rest of the film, has a potluck quality that is definitely strained. It has something to do with three clientless lawyers and two comedians in need of legal advice about breaking their eleven-year nightclub contract. Contact is made, and pies start flying. And suddenly there is a grand finale, with Carmen Amaya. The King Cole Trio, Yvette and a group of tumblers called the Cristiania, appearing in violent and rather disjointed succession.

If the unnamed reviewer expected more from the manic Olsen and Johnson team, this evaluator needed to attend another movie with other comedians. Ole and Chic traded in the chaotic and did have a following for many years.

Ed Hartmann scripted only one picture, *The Caddy* (1953), for the comedy team of Dean Martin and Jerry Lewis. One probably could have been enough. As previously indicated fledgling writer Danny Arnold became a sycophant for Jerry and this political situation caused some problems in the completion of the creative process. Lewis, himself, would have been enough of a problem. In a 1986 interview for Canadian television, Ed set forth this perceptive view on a man with great potential: His ego plus drive to be the star got in the way.

The Caddy employs the similar characters of previous movies. Jerry Lewis enacts the role of a case of arrested development and Dean Martin a suave, man-about-town—an incredible contrast in persona, in some respects a shadow of the past, the straight man and the comic. Much like Abbott and Costello. In fact Martin and Lewis received recognition for the service comedy, a decade after Bud and Lou's move from burlesque to motion pictures. Three humorous films with a military theme were, *At War with the Army* (1950), *Sailor Beware* (1951), and *Jumping Jacks* (1952). As with most comedians it was necessary to develop plots using various professions, locations, and endeavors. Show business remains a focus since comedy routines, song, and dance numbers were the forte of Martin and Lewis. Even *The Caddy* begins with the two men engaged in professional golf contests to professional stage shows.

As a son of a golf pro, Harvey Miller Jr. (Jerry Lewis) knows enough about the game to appoint himself as a manager and teacher. He becomes very obnoxious when he gives instructions to Ben Hogan, a pro of the period playing himself for the film. Part of the humor of the comedian's character develops from his good intentions but obtrusive attempts to help professional golfers as well as a would-be rising golf star, Dean Martin as Joe Anthony in this movie. This aspect of the film does work. Two other routines by Lewis seem forced. Jerry's feigned bit as a sophisticated gentleman and an occasional overstatement of his mentally dense character misfires.

Jerry Lewis imitates a high society person that becomes a caricature of an artist or British aristocrat. He dons a smoking jacket with a scarf for a tie and smokes a cigarette in a long holder. He uses this disguise to impress people at the country club noted for its important golf tournaments. Even if this ruse were an effective comic routine—and it isn't—it is improbable that such a dope as Harvey could even come close to acting this way. An initial development of Harvey's character shows him half-awakened from a sleep. He puts on some clothes and staggers away with contortions of his mouth and body as if he were a mental defective from birth. Furthermore, Jerry lapses into this mode, with a little more restraint, when he is fully awake. The sleepwalking saved us from the voice because it was executed in pantomime. Jerry's whine and a shrill yapping in a mock version of a child's voice passes for comedy. It is a standard part of his comedy and when he changes to the sophisticate using something close to his own voice it is hard to suspend belief that he is consistent in his comic character. However, there are moments in *The Caddy* when Lewis has effective routines.

Jerry handles a comic drunk to produce some effective laughter. To keep Dean (Joe) in training for a golf tournament, he keeps him from drinking by stealing the glass before he can pick it up. After consuming many glasses of liquor the comedian staggers through the clubhouse rooms knocking over anything in his path. Broad slapstick, of course, but well performed. And, as previously mentioned, his comedy of the obnoxious attempts to give advice to golf pros does provide satisfactory humor. It is possible that writers Hartmann and Ken Englund realized one of Lewis's real-life facets, rude intrusions, provided material for the character of Harvey in *The Caddy*.

While Ed had high opinion of some comic actors who he worked with, Olsen and Johnson, Bob Hope, and William Demarest, he had penetrating insight on the nature of many comedians. Ed observed, "Most comics are paranoid and very mean spirited. That's the right word. And so insecure, and so . . . well, when you see a group of comics together they generally don't listen to each other. They wait in silence as they're thinking up a joke. Then they'll pop in with their joke at the first opportunity. Then stop listening. They're not good company."

Edmund might have been thinking of Jerry Lewis; however, when he elaborated later in an interview he tempered his analysis. He saw Jerry's ego and drive for success and attention obstructing his goal. When Dean and Jerry broke up, fate played a strange trick. It was thought Martin would fade and Lewis would be a big star. "Dean could care less," Edmund commented, "A golf game, a drink or a pretty girl was all he cared about. And it all came to him. Where Jerry, seeking desperately for it, never could quite catch it."

Since I had spent decades studying comedy I was amazed when Ed said succinctly what I saw as the comedian's inability to judge his own work.

"He had a marvelous talent which could be harnessed if he could only find someone he could listen to. Some mentor who said 'Do this   don't do this.' I think he would have been one of the biggest comics next to Chaplin."

Hartmann expressed it so well. When Lewis thought he could direct his own pictures, his films diminished with each of his efforts. His movies proved to be so weak in the late '80s he could no longer get the backing of a major studio. And, of course, an American tragedy can happen even to a comedian.

Posed comic publicity photo for Jane Russell and Bob Hope film *The Paleface* (1948). (From the collection of Donald McCaffrey)

Hedy Lamarr portrays a femme fatale in Hope's intrigue comedy *My Favorite Spy* (1951). (From the collection of Donald McCaffrey)

During the Hollywood struggle with censorship from the House Un-American Activities Committee, Ed became the leader of the Screen Writers Guild, West. (From the collection of Ed Hartmann)

President Hartmann (far left) heads a meeting with some of the most famous members of the Screen Writers Guild. (From the collection of Ed Hartmann)

Fred MacMurray, star of the long-running series *My Three Sons*, talks with Ed. (From the collection of Ed Hartmann)

Henry Fonda appeared as the lead in the short-lived *The Smith Family* television series. (From the collection of Donald McCaffrey)

Three of the original cast in the television series *Family Affair*. From left to right: Anissa Jones (holding her doll), Sebastian Cabot, and Johnny Whittaker. A revival of the series premiered in September 2002. (From the collection of Donald McCaffrey)

Nearly thirty years after the demise of *Family Affair*, the Mrs. Beasley doll made a nostalgic reincarnation to adults in the newspaper supplements of Sunday, October 14, 2001. (From the collection of Donald McCaffrey)

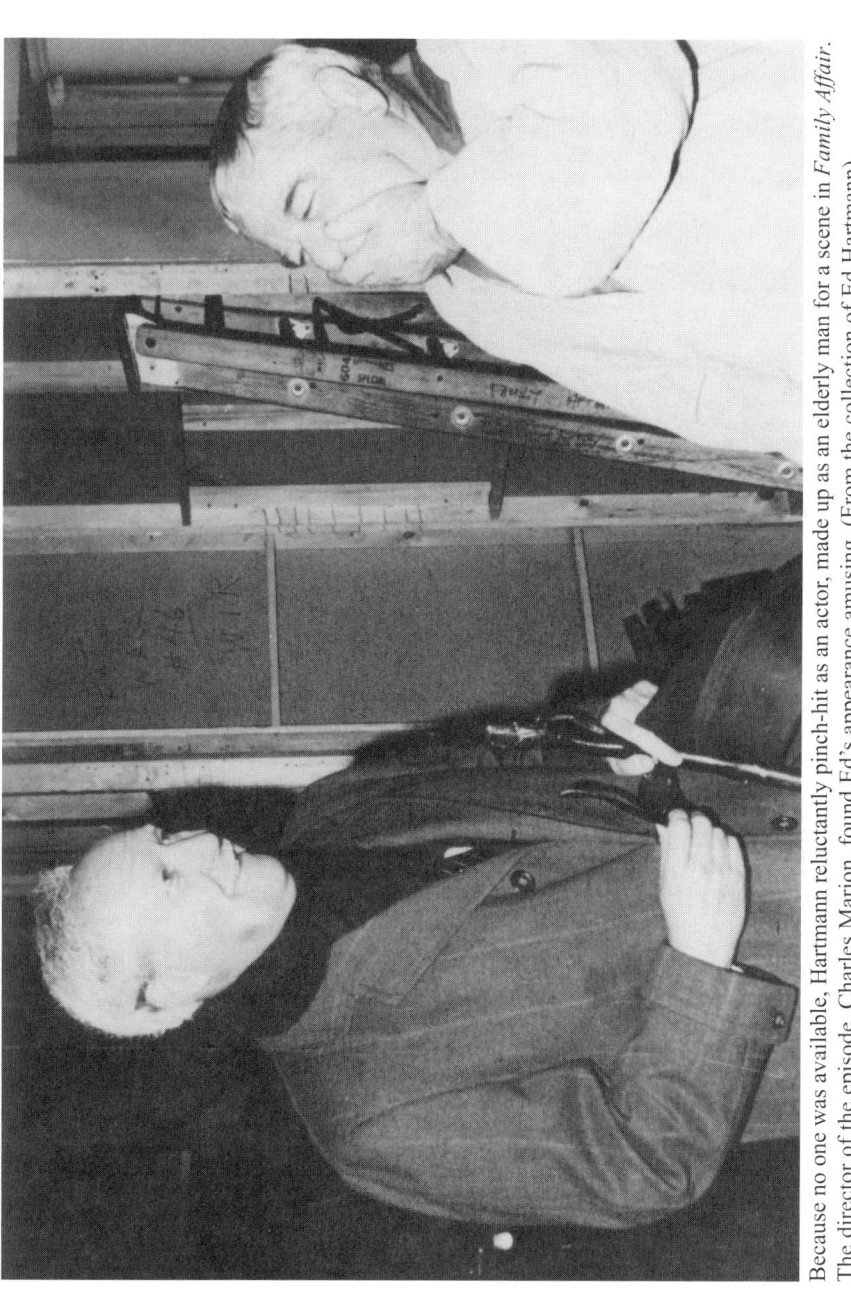

Because no one was available, Hartmann reluctantly pinch-hit as an actor, made up as an elderly man for a scene in *Family Affair*. The director of the episode, Charles Marion, found Ed's appearance amusing. (From the collection of Ed Hartmann)

presents

Nanette Fabray

in

A New and Original Comedy
especially written for
Nanette Fabray

"The Oscar Ladies"

by Edmund Hartmann

October 7 - November 1

Ed wrote a stage show for Nanette Fabray called *The Oscar Ladies*, giving the comedienne the opportunity to play five roles. (From the collection of Ed Hartmann)

6
Thanks for the Memories: There was Hope

In my interview with Hartmann I witnessed how he reflected on the memories of his association with Bob Hope. Some of his most successful creations evolved when Ed wrote seven screenplays for the comedian during his long association with Paramount. He also took a minor stab at writing for Bob on a multiple scripted movie with a number of writers. He may have handled a brief golf sketch, a cameo, with Bing Crosby for the 1947 *Variety Girl*. As one of four screenwriters in the studio's potpourri of leading actors and extras Edmund Hartmann's contribution is not clear. So this picture was obviously not one of Ed's main Hope pictures. However, he wrote scripts for *The Paleface* (1948), *Sorrowful Jones* (1949), *Fancy Pants* (1950), *The Lemon Drop Kid* (1951), *My Favorite Spy* (1951), *Here Come the Girls* (1953), and *Casanova's Big Night* (1954).

Memories of his association with Bob persisted as he recalled the positive writing that exhibited some of the best of his total career.

His first film with Paramount, *Variety Girl*, became an assignment to broadcast the extent of the studio's talent—proving that this company ranked with MGM. *Variety Girl* as a movie actually preexisted as a stage show. When Bob Hope took the position as Master of Ceremonies in the stage version, he deftly introduced stars who were the cream of Paramount Studio. The actors presented comedy sketches or musical numbers. Of Hope's role in this stage presentation Ed remarked, "I saw him do an entire benefit for the variety club when we did the *Variety Girl*. And he knew nothing about who was on or anything else. He had no rehearsals. Paramount Theater—a jammed theatre. He walked in at the back. There was a man waiting for him with a list of the cast. He took that list, walked out on the stage, and you would have thought he rehearsed that show for six weeks. He was so at ease, he was so funny; he was so wonderful in introducing those people. He was completely in charge of the entire evening. He was fantastic!"

"The interesting thing about *Paleface*," Edmund reminisced, "We [Ed, Jack Rose, and Frank Tashlin] were under contract with Paramount to do a show. They called us in and said they wanted a Western with Hope and Jane Russell. That was the only assignment. We went up to our office and talked about the possibilities and all. And I came up with the story of Calamity Jane. We told it to the head of the studio, Frank Butler. He said, 'No, it will never work. No way.' He burst into the office about ten minutes later and said, 'I got it, boys!' and told us the same story exactly. Exactly, no change at all. I said, 'That's great!' So we did it."

The Paleface became the first of the genre that spawned three other Hope Westerns—*Fancy Pants, Son of Paleface,* and *Alias Jesse James.* Of the four pictures Hartmann's *The Paleface* and *Fancy Pants* now are realized as superior to the latter two.

The Paleface became one of the highest grossing films of the year. It was a picture that has been reported to top most of Hope's movies—seven million dollars. The comedian, with Hartmann's excellent script, was provided a vehicle to show Hope's ability to display comic meekness, cowardly withdrawal under stress, and pretension to manliness in an attempt to con his enemies. Jane Russell proved to be a counterpoint to his character. She possessed no fear and usually was in control of any situation—a comic inversion of the typical mild supporter-of-the-male type of woman in the Western. In the exposition of the story, Calamity Jane is released from jail and given a pardon if she will hunt down the traders giving guns to the Indians. The opening scenes exist in the world of melodrama until Bob Hope appears as Painless Peter Potter, a fledgling dentist seeking clients in the land of rugged men and women far from the eastern world.

The movie audience sees Peter, the hapless beginner, frequently referring to a guidebook to his trade. He has a customer who proves to be a surly Westerner with a toothache. With the thug's mouth wide open, Peter's bow tie drops into the patient's mouth. Observing that he has a tie just like it, the bungler is startled and does a double-take as he realizes *it is his.* Using the anesthesia called laughing gas employed by dentists in that period of history, the patient asks if it is safe. Potter says, "Safest thing in the world. Would you mind paying me now?" In the confusion this amateur, who Calamity calls Painless, pulls the wrong tooth and laughs about it since he receives a whiff of the laughing gas he is using for an anesthetic. The tough declares, "I'll give you just fifteen minutes to get out of town!" Using his perfect, one-beat timing, Hope says, "Last town they gave me twenty minutes." And both men are laughing from the gas between carping insults directed at each other.

People watching this film today or even in 1948 or 1949 may have had little historical perspective of the many dentist chair lampoons that existed in the '20s and '30s. For example, W. C. Fields wrote and acted in a number of Mack Sennett's early two-reel sound films, and one of them, *The Dentist* (1932), burlesqued a trip to the dentist. Fields displayed a nonplussed attitude as he applied his trade. Although he is bewildered with the negative reactions of his patients, he plows ahead as if he knows what he's doing. Bob Hope's Peter Potter exists on the opposite of the pole. His character is a meek, hesitant soul who is easily flustered when he has to handle nervous and demanding patients. The comedy develops from a man who does not have the aggressiveness in the world of the bold and brave.

In a well-plotted story, Painless Potter mistakenly believes he has superior power as a sharpshooter when attacked by Indians. While he shoots at the invading horde, it is the crack-shot Calamity who is dispatching the Indians out of Peter's vision. She mows them down one at a time.

Hope as Potter has two important sequences when he pretends to be another person. When Calamity dispatches Indians on the attack, Painless mistakenly becomes the hero of the moment. Even the people in this little frontier town believe he is the hero who stopped the attack of the Indians. So, he tries to become a tough cowboy. He invests in a very showy cowboy outfit that only could be worn by an outsider—what would be called a "tenderfoot" imitation of a cowhand. Then he thinks he is manly when he struts around the town affecting a deeper voice with an added Western twang. His posturing creates a parody of a champion. A combination of melodramatic plotting and humorous reactions by comedian Hope helped move the climactic sequence effectively to *The Paleface*'s conclusion. Director McLeod accelerated the pace in this latter portion of the film. Many of the clichés of the stock Western plot evolved to provide an intriguing comic ending. With ceremony the villainous gang of white men bring dynamite and rifles to the Indians. In league with the exploiting mob, the natives capture both Calamity and Potter. Tied to a stake, the aggressive Jane becomes helpless as she is about to go up in flames like Joan of Arc. Potter escapes and comes back to rescue Calamity. He is hesitant to save her because he fears what may happen to him if he is caught in Medicine Man's attire. Some of the best comedy develops with his reaction to a proposed heroic attempt to save Jane. A voice-over argument with his inner thoughts portrays a humorous debate of the pros and cons of a plan of action. His love for Calamity emboldens the meek part of his character.

He outwits both the Indians and the villains by using powder for the guns to set off the dynamite. Potter and Jane escape in an elaborate chase scene that has the couple pursued by the natives, and the wagon used for their wild ride is loaded with explosives. There is a switch to the final resolution of the film as we see the couple married and ready to go on a honeymoon. Calamity insists on taking the reins of the horses drawing Potter's dental wagon. The horses break away, dragging Jane behind them. Hope executes a camera take and declares, "What do you want, a happy ending?"

An Oscar-winning song, "Buttons and Bows," in the film seems to be tossed off as Hope delivers it with a concertina. With tongue in cheek, critic Bosley Crowther wrote, "The great things in human progress—and in art— usually happen this way. 'The Paleface' deserves primarily a marker as the birthplace of 'Buttons and Bows'" (*New York Times*, December 18, p.41). Crowther becomes more clever than correct. He viewed this picture on the same level as the five "Road" movies that preceded this movie—of which the first, *The Road to Singapore,* appeared eight years earlier, in 1940. *Time* and other critics rank this Western comedy starring Bob Hope as one the actor's best. And

"Buttons and Bows" became a hit of the year.

And this was not the end of *The Paleface*. Twenty years later Edmund Hartmann and Frank Tashlin received credit for a version of the film entitled *The Shakiest Gun in the West*. This 1968 remake of Hartmann's very successful picture starred Don Knotts, and did not make the grade as did the Hope picture. The latter day version of the hapless dentist left much to be desired when it is compared with the 1948 original. While Hartmann and Tashlin are given credit for the basic story, screenwriters Jim Fritzell and Everett Greenbaum are in larger letters above the original screenwriters in the opening credits, "Based on the screenplay of Edmund Hartmann and Frank Tashlin." Most "based on" creations of a screenplay or novel often mean "suggested by." And so a picture for Hope, transformed into a picture for Don Knotts, suffered a strange sea change. The standard comedy of Knotts showed his character in constant stress and frustration. It was a portrait of a wimp struggling in the world bent on crushing him. Unlike Hope, who gave comic characters with a dimension that changed from picture to picture from the con man to the man conned—from a happy-go-lucky person who can weather many storms to a person full of fear when villains pursue him. Unlike Knotts, who quakes and stutters when confronted, Hope tries to hide his anxiety even though the audience realizes he is extremely disturbed.

Screenwriters Fritzell and Greenbaum used a thin thread of the plot-line used by the originators of *The Paleface*. They made the mistake of trying to add new situations to fit comedian Knotts—with the intention of improving on the original version. A similar attempt developed when Frank Tashlin took the reins of a sequel, *Son of Paleface*, in 1952. When I asked Hartmann why he didn't create a script for this Bob Hope movie he replied simply, "They didn't ask me." It is more likely that Tashlin convinced Paramount he could write and direct the picture on his own. Being a gag writer and director of Warner Brothers cartoons did not equip Frank to handle live action features such as *Son of Paleface*. With an ability to monitor his own comic skills, Hope gave an outstanding portrait of the son of Peter Potter. However, the minimal acting skills of Jane Russell and Roy Rogers needed a director who helped with the success of *The Paleface*, Norman Z. McLeod. Tashlin could not get much of a performance from Russell or Rogers, whose thespian abilities were about as advanced as his role as a singing cowboy in most of his films. Furthermore, Frank's screenwriting lacked the coherence of story lines produced by Ed Hartmann for the 1948 original. Nevertheless, Bob Hope's performance does make *Son of Paleface* worth watching.

Fortunately, Hartmann's screenwriting helped make the 1950 *Fancy Pants* an effective vehicle for comedian Hope. But director George Marshall proved to be one of Ed's least favorite associates in the development of a major work the screenwriter had created. Hartmann related how he had written a monologue for the leading actor.

"Hope is in a picture called *Fancy Pants*—which I wrote. Bob Welch produced it. There was a scene of a cricket match. George Marshall, an old mean son-of-a-bitch, was director. Producer Welch did *The Paleface* and this was only his second picture. After we did that, we were doing *Fancy Pants*. There were maybe fifty tables around the cricket field. I had a monologue for Hope. The day before I told it to Welch and he loved it. But he said we had to shoot it the next day. We stayed up late working on the monologue. The director comes on the field the next day and Welch comes up to him and told him it was the monologue to be shot this day. So, Marshall, being the real prick, takes it and doesn't look at it. He says, 'I've written some things on the back of the envelope and that's what we're going to do today.' He takes my script and throws it on the table. After some of the cricket scene was shot there was a break to set the lights and camera for more shooting. Hope sat down at the table and saw the script. Picks it up and reads it. 'Hey, this is great. This is very funny.' He calls Marshall and says, 'Let's do this. It's great!' Marshall says, 'What's this?'—pretending to have never seen it. Marshall reads it and said, 'That's very funny. Yeah.' They did it. By sheer accident of Hope sitting down at this one table." It was fate and this scene in the movie later illustrated how adept the comedian was in handling a long monologue. This tall tale created by Hartmann comes in the first portion of the movie. It is developed in the sequence when an actor, who on stage enacts the role of an English butler, is hired by a ranch family in the western part of the United States. Hope plays a deception role as a person called Humphrey who must convince the naïve people of this little town that he is an Earl from England. He decides to impress the crowd of listeners that he has had many dangerous adventures in the British army.

Hope gives a version of the pending extreme danger as natives in India stop their drum beat—indicating they are about to attack. "Trying to wipe us out, you know. But they were only waiting for the end of the monsoons." He relates with some confusing details as he continues and then indicates his plight became greater. Humphrey continues, "Those infernal drums cease. Imagine it, three against a thousand."

Hope, the not-so-magnificent pretender, then explains how other danger in the jungle presented other threats—"vicious crocodiles and hissing pythons."

At one point in the narration, Humphrey receives a missile from the enemy, "I had a spear right through my body." He pantomimes pulling out the spear and retaliates with slashing movements as if he hacks away with a cutlass. With Hope's comic beat of a second, he explains that he must take a nap "before going to sleep."

The townspeople ask what happened.

Humphrey off-handedly says, "We finally put them to rout. But we all agreed they were the three toughest rascals we had ever fought. Goodnight, goodnight."

After the repetition of "three against a thousand" Hartmann's punch line provides a startling comic reversal. Hope's underplaying of the conclusion of the tall tale puts an effective cap on the pretender. Especially notable is the comedian's ability to blend the verbal with the physical. With the help of Lucille Ball, playing the part of Aggie, the daughter of the ranch owner, Hope enacts the con man actor who has been hired to improve the manners of both Aggie and the ranch owner, Mike. This is designed by Mrs. Effie Floud, the wife of Mike and an assertive matron who wants to impress the citizens of Big Squaw by being the leader in the community. Effie, thereby, becomes the pretender because her efforts become comically inadequate. The same can be said of Humphrey's deception as a person who doesn't really comprehend the manners of an Englishman.

Broader humor that reaches a slapstick level develops when the western townsfolk attempt to engage in a fox hunt using a curious collection of every size and breed of dog in the town. Seeing he has a rival for the hand of Aggie, the town bully Cart Belknap (played by actor Bruce Cabot—noted for roles as villains) smears gravy on Humphrey's fox hunt riding-coat. Consequently, the band of dogs smell the gravy and chase the servant pretender who also tries to pass as an Earl. Another chase scene evolves when both Aggie and Humphrey try to retrieve an album containing the stage notices of Hope's role as an actor in the first sequence of the film. Since the actor is exposed as a fraud, the couple express their love for each other and must go to another town.

One odd final gag in the movie shows Humphrey and Aggie fleeing from Big Squaw as they pump up and down on a two-person railroad car. As they enter a tunnel, a train roars through it. Then, the two are shown pumping up and down as they travel on a car split in half. What is called the fantastic gag is a refurbished concluding gag from the two-reel Laurel and Hardy movie, *Two Tars*.

Of the four Hope Westerns, the 1959 *Alias Jessie James* is the weakest entry. The premise of the picture has potential. Hope as the insurance salesman named Milford Farnsworth sells a $100,000 policy to Jesse James, but must see that James lives or his company faces bankruptcy. Jesse has the brilliant idea of getting Milford to impersonate him in order to collect the insurance. While this plot entanglement provides enough comic intrigue, the handling of the film faced the problem of an inadequate script, director, and actors. Even Hope seems to be lackluster in his portrait after turning in excellent work with *The Paleface, Fancy Pants,* and *Son of Paleface.* A cracking and fizzling fire entered his comic repertoire and muted his performance. It is possible that Wendell Corey's weary portrait of a comic villain didn't gel. An actor like Bruce Cabot from *Fancy Pants* might have remedied the quality of the total picture. Bob Hope did his best when he had an actor with charisma—especially his works with Lucille Ball. What is surprising about the directing, by Norman Z. McLeod, is his previous handling of *The Paleface*, Hope's most successful film in his career—both critical and financial. Part of the director's problem remains the lack of effective screenwriters. He needed such scripters as Ed Hartmann, Hal Kanter, and Robert O'Brien. More and more the top writers were moving to television from Hollywood where they had more control of their teleplays.

Paramount created refurbished versions of pictures released fifteen or twenty years after these movies were successful in the '30s. This practice gave Hartmann an opportunity to adapt two character developed works for Hope that illustrated the actor's ability to execute a basically serious role with strong comic touches. In 1934 Paramount cast Adolph Menjou and Shirley Temple in the leading roles of Damon Runyon's short story "Little Miss Marker." This version of the tale of a racetrack tout, played by Menjou, emphasizes the serious and sentimental that often received a blending in a Runyon work. The same year another racetrack con man from another story by this same author featured Lee Tracy in the film adaptation, *The Lemon Drop Kid.* It became obvious that the two films had to be tailored for the talents of Bob Hope. The remake of *Little Miss Marker,* retiled *Sorrowful Jones,* received its release in 1949, a year later than the Hope-Hartmann *The Paleface.* Retaining the original title of *The Lemon Drop Kid,* Hope once more enacted the part of a racetrack con man.

The 1934 Damon Runyon film adaptations employed leading men, Menjou and Tracy, who played both serious and light comedy roles. But they were not noted as comedians, per se. Hope, on the other hand, was considered confined to comic portraits. Later in the 50s Hope would take a bold step into even more serious dramas with some urging from screenwriters Jack Rose and Melville Shavelson to handle the famous vaudevillian Eddie Foy in the 1955 *The Seven Little Foys.* Hope returned to a more serious portrayal in 1957 in the film *Beau James,* depicting a likable rogue, Jimmy Walker, mayor of New York City. Both of these acting assignments indicated that Bob could depict the darker side of a man who came close to a picaresque character.

Hope's 1949 creation of Sorrowful Jones did not have the sting of his Eddie Foy. In his relationship with his children and adults, Foy could be not only sarcastic he could be cruel. Sorrowful Jones proved to be stingy and self-centered —a type of mild rogue or picaresque person—but he melted under the influence of a little girl for whom he was forced to become a surrogate father. Her real father was killed by a gang who, like the Mafia, would shoot a man who tried to wiggle out of a debt. Sorrowful eventually became a soft touch when "little Miss Marker," whose real name was Martha Jane Smith, made him kneel down for a goodnight prayer. Ed Hartmann told me how the script called for the girl to include a racehorse called Dreamy Joe and Sorrowful in her plea for God's blessing and a gift. Mary Jane asks God to give Sorrowful a new suit. Ed told me he gave Hope a line for this scene to cap the bookie's parsimonious trait. This con man added to the request, "With two pair of pants, please." This addition indicates one of the character's comic deviations from the norm—his tightfisted and grasping attributes. Actress Lucille Ball as Gladys in the exposition of *Sorrowful Jones* ridicules him with sarcasm. As Sorrowful views a female manikin in a store window, she suggests he take "the dummy" to dinner because she doesn't eat. His stingy nature is pointed out by Gladys when she takes another dig at his excessively frugal nature, "You know it's been almost four years since I saw you, Sorrowful, but I recognize the suit." Feebly he tries to indicate it is his suit with a charm, "It's been lucky for me—up to now. Some people seem to forget what some people spend on some people." Gladys tops the conversation with the last statements, "Spend? Where did you ever learn that word? I always figured you invented the Dutch treat." In the role of Gladys, Lucille Ball contributes effectively as a female foil. Lucille became one of the best coleads for Bob. Her comic flair the next year, 1950 as a ranch daughter in the Southwest would show how she had the ingenious ability to switch the humorous portrait from picture to picture. It was the same talent Hope possessed. And, Miss Ball proved to be a woman superior to all others when she was teamed with Hope in such pictures as *The Facts of Life* (1960). Like her role in *Sorrowful Jones* there is displayed the drama of pithy, witty lines.

Another version of the Runyon "Little Miss Marker" story employed the popular actor Walter Matthau in the role of Sorrowful Jones, a film that, in 1980, relied on the original title of *Little Miss Marker*. It provides an excellent example of how screenwriters tailored the story and situations to fit the comedian. Bob Hope never depicted the role of a curmudgeon. Matthau, on the other hand, used this portrait as his mainstay as a comic actor. Walter as Sorrowful would be one to hold out before he melted under the charms of the little girl, often referred to as "The Kid." Hope became an easier touch in the 1949 version with Hartmann's script.

Some of the best humor that avoids the potential sentimentality of the theme comes from the persistent hanging on to Sorrowful by the little girl, played by Viola Kates Simpson. Scriptwriter and director Walter Bernstein seems to draw the model of The Kid from the Jackie Coogan boy character in Charlie Chaplin's 1921 *The Kid*. Somewhat like The Little Tramp for which Chaplin became famous, Walter Matthau reluctantly becomes the surrogate father for the little girl. The Kid in the '80s *Little Miss Marker* has some of the resolute quality of Coogan's Kid or the little adult stubbornness to overcome obstacles. The girl actress Viola Simpson almost takes scenes from veteran comedian Matthau. Bob Hope holds his own with the child actress. Notably absent is the cynical woman portrayal of Lucille Ball in *Sorrowful Jones*. Instead, Julie Andrews seems to be engaged in a reprisal of her 1964 title role Mary Poppins in the movie. She gives advice to Sorrowful and even takes the male role of proposing marriage. Once again, though without the magical powers of the unusual nanny, she is a Miss Fixit and romantic interest for curmudgeon Matthau. As in the Hope and Ball movie, the couples marry for a happy-ever-after resolution. For the best humor of these two versions, the Hope/Hartmann version of the character of Sorrowful makes the more effective movie.

Hartmann's 1951 release of another Damon Runyon screenplay featured Hope as another racetrack tout, named Sidney Melbourne but better known as the Lemon Drop Kid after his habit of popping the confection instead of pills. Edmund Hartmann developed a Runyon portrait that doesn't have the dimension of Sorrowful Jones, however the picture possesses enough intrigue and comic character to be one of the appealing channels for Hope's talents.

The basic plot shows the Kid almost hopelessly in debt to a mob that relishes manipulations of horse races. Since he must pay the boss, Moose Moran, thousands of dollars, Sidney develops a scam tied to Christmas charity. The idea for this ruse develops when he observes street corner bell ringing men dressed in Santa Claus suits. The Kid recruits a group of unkempt roughnecks for the role of charity bell ringers. He knows a motherly street paper saleswoman who wants to retire to what Sidney called Nellie Thursday's Home for "Old Dolls."

The bookie from the racetrack in *The Lemon Drop Kid* cannot resist temptation. When he sees the money flowing in from the Santa Claus kettles, he must abscond with the cash. The Kid's girlfriend Brainy Baxter, a part enacted by Marilyn Maxwell, convinces him that he must carry out his promise to the boarding home for elderly ladies who most have outlived their husbands. Unfortunately Brainy's boss, Charlie, at the nightclub where she is a torch singer, sees the scam as a way to line his own pockets. He uses the same device promoted by the Kid and even moves the home for "Old Dolls."

Complications develop as both Moose and Charlie vie for the scam. On the side of Nellie Thursday and her women, the Kid dresses up as an Old Doll in order to steal the money owed to the ladies.

He grabs the money bag full of thousands of dollars from Charlie in the final climactic chase of the movie. There is a resolution to the whole comic drama with a celebration of the women who have a home saved from the greed of both Moose and Charlie.

One unusual aspect of *The Lemon Drop Kid* is the hit song of "Silver Bells" by composer songwriters Jay Livingston and Ray Evans, the same songsmiths who received recognition for "Buttons and Bows" for Hope and Hartmann's *The Paleface* only three years earlier. According to Ed Hartmann, Ray Evans lived well on the royalties for the Yuletide hit, "Silver Bells." In fact, *The Lemon Drop Kid* with Bob Hope plays on television during the Christmas season at the same time that Jimmy Stewart appears on television in Frank Capra's Christmas-themed *It's a Wonderful Life* (1946).

Hartmann told me an anecdote about the Livingston and Evans choice for a title for the popular Christmas song. Their first name was "Tinkle Bells," However, Jay Livingston's wife suggested a change by saying, "You know what tinkle is?" While Hope and Maxwell sang the duet of "Silver Bells," ironically they were not featured in the release of the record. Bob's partner in the Road pictures, Bing Crosby, because he was the most popular male vocalist of the middle of the twentieth century, received the privilege and the royalties.

The Lemon Drop Kid did not have the distinction of a leading character played by Hope that could match his role of Sorrowful in the previous Damon Runyon movie. Hartmann evidently tried to give the Kid a distinct personality in an elaborate introduction of Sidney:

1. Onlookers at a Florida racetrack observe the Kid talking to a racehorse. The horse whinnies and he interprets the meaning of the horse's communication to him as if there is a tip on which horse will win in the next race. Two policemen approach and threaten to take him away. He talks them out of an arrest with a con man's plea of innocence.
2. He wanders the crowd of people who are waiting for the race to begin and gives two couples a tip on the next contest. Obviously naïve, each couple receives separate tips. Because they are told there will be big winnings, they say they will share their money with him. He tells a man and women that his share will go to a clinic for horses that are too ill to enter a race. He fills out his scorecard so that one of his bogus tips will give him a winner.
3. He gives the wrong tip to a woman who is a girlfriend of Moose Moran. Since the horse does not win, the Kid must pay ten thousand dollars that the horse would have brought in as the winner.

Despite this elaborate exposition that developed Sidney Melbourne's character, his persona as a con man did not develop as well as the Hope/Hartmann Sorrowful Jones. In this second Hartmann/Damon Runyon screen adaptation, The Kid doesn't show a side of having to deal with a moppet, but he does deal with elderly women and exhibits a soft side that contrasts with his con man demeanor. Hope and Lucille Ball engaged in banter that added dimension to their portraits. Sorrowful becomes more than a con man. He often is humiliated when Gladys jokingly cuts him down with a sarcastic remark. With the casting of Marilyn Maxwell as the romantic interest for Sidney, Hope doesn't have the competition when a woman plays a straight role. Miss Ball, whenever she is cast with Hope, adds comic spice to their movies. And she received a costarring role with him in four films: *Sorrowful Jones, Fancy Pants, The Facts of Life* (1960), and *Critic's Choice* (1962).

According to Ed Hartmann he beefed-up the role and dialogue for Hedy Lamarr as Lily Dalbray in the 1951 *My Favorite Spy*. She did not play a straight role like Marilyn Maxwell in *The Lemon Drop Kid*. Lamarr enacted a parody of a beautiful, sexy siren, they type of role she was better noted for.

In the opening scene of *My Favorite Spy,* Bob Hope is detained by police because he bears a striking resemblance to an international spy, Eric Augustine. Out of his third-rate burlesque costume, Peanuts White looks exactly like the spy who is associated with Lily Dalbray. Augustine is a suave lover and Lily exists as a female sophisticate with all the charms of a Jezebel-like spy. Prodded and flattered into becoming an imitator and operative double of Eric Augustine, Peanuts receives elaborate training from the U.S. government. He looks at movies of the spy whose movements and total demeanor he will copy. A number of attractive women become the object of practice kisses. He perfects this skill to the point that a lady's hose develops runs from the passion he evokes. Dressed as Eric Augustine, he is the debonair man who wears silk stockings. He meets a very cool but sexy Lily, kisses her fervently. A close-up of his hose shows runs are created from her passionate return of his embrace. He looks down at her legs and sees no runs.

Throughout his encounter with Lily in Tangiers, he is capable of imitating Augustine with some skill with a few comic lapses, but we see him as a coward when he realizes someone is trying to assassinate him. Peanuts immediately starts packing a suitcase and calls to book a flight on an airplane to the United States. He finds that he has many difficulties leaving Tangiers when international assassins are pursuing him and the real Eric Augustine. They kill Eric and Peanuts sees the body of the man he has been imitating. Hope delivers one of the best lines of the script as he observes the dead Eric, "Ach du lieber, Augustine," which is a word play on a popular German child's song that many of the audience in the early '50s would likely have recognized.

One of the highlights of Hope's ability to deliver a monologue plus physical comic gestures to fit a series of impersonations evolves when he is captured by a group of espionage plotters. Peanuts is given a truth serum that is designed to get secrets from the bogus Augustine. When the drug takes effect, he starts out with a song and dance. Then he portrays a series of stage characters that provides a gamut of his wacky versions of Cyrano de Bergerac, the ghoulish Hyde from Robert Lewis Stevenson's *The Strange Case of Dr. Jekyll and Mr. Hyde*, and a burlesque of Hamlet. What is important about *My Favorite Spy* is it shows the versatility of Bob Hope as a comedian. Fulfilling the line from Shakespeare's *As You Like It*, he proved within his life and career he was a human who "played many parts." In *My Favorite Spy* he played the buffoon trying his best to be a burlesque clown who achieved success with his audiences. Seduced by a government that needed him to assume a role of a spy, he did rise above its expectations. Of course, the part he played had flaws, especially his inability to play the cool, relentless hero. However good luck saw him through and he won the woman, Lily, at the end of the many intrigues of the spy movie. Thus, Hope played three parts: Peanuts, the third-rate burlesque actor, Augustine, the smooth, sophisticated spy, and his carbon copy of Eric. These three roles were well established and created by Hope.

During World War II Hollywood released a rash of intrigue comedies. Bob was cast in three of these works are tied to the thriller genre besides *My Favorite Spy*: *You Got Me Covered* (1942), *My Favorite Blonde* (1942), and *My Favorite Brunette* (1947). The 1942 releases were not authored by Hartmann, but did have roles for Hope to show his comic versatility. Both screenwriter and actor achieved some of their best work in the decades of the '40s and '50s. *You Got Me Covered* and *My Favorite Blonde* focused on the spy comedy that depicted international saboteurs and obsessively crazy characters, Otto Preminger and Donald Meek in the former with Gale Sondergaard and George Zucco in the latter. Such villainous caricatures provide humorous scenes as the comic hero struggles to avoid capture and torture.

The risible plot and dialogue of the screenwriters plus the performances of the actors of *My Favorite Blonde* make this picture the equal of the Hope/Hartmann *My Favorite Spy*. The combination of Hope and Madeleine Carroll has some of the magic of casting Hope with Lucille Ball. Somewhat similar to the Hartmann scripted *My Favorite Spy*, Hope is a sucker for the ravishing Carroll instead of Hedy Lamarr.

It may be that *My Favorite Blonde* is superior to Hartmann's *My Favorite Spy*. Part of the reason this evaluation can be made is the fact that Madeleine Carroll also played the lead woman in Alfred Hitchcock's *The 39 Steps*, so she understood the spoof on this melodrama, which made substantial use of humor itself. But she also had experience in a number of light comedies when she came to the United States in the late '30s. Paramount cast her as the costar with Fred MacMurray in 1939 in *Honeymoon in Bali* and *Cafe Society*, and then in 1941 they appeared together in *One Night in Lisbon* and *Virginia*.

As much as Ed Hartmann gave Hedy Lamarr a stronger personality as a take-off on the vamp plus comic dialogue in *My Favorite Spy*, she had only moments that made her the match of the Bob and Madeleine duo in *My Favorite Blonde*.

In Hope's career he created some of his best movies from the '40s to the '50s, in the period adventure comedies. He developed the leading character in three works of this genre: *The Princess and the Pirate* (1944), *Monsieur Beaucaire* (1946), and *Casanova's Big Night* (1954). Some might classify the genre as linked to the Western because of its historical roots; however the Western story has been set mainly in the nineteenth century. The movement from the settled east to the west became a special focus that developed the legends celebrated in popular literature and the motion pictures.

The period adventure comedy often reflects the culture in European or Mediterranean countries during the seventeenth and eighteenth centuries. The Ed Hartmann and Hal Kanter script of *Casanova's Big Night* employs an opening narration that sets the location in Italy in the year 1757. *Monsieur Beaucaire*, with a screenplay by Melvin Frank and Norman Panama, places the event of the drama in France during the reign of Louis XVI. Therefore, both comedies create the world of the eighteenth century. Also, the leading characters played by Bob Hope impersonate royalty while they are only commoners. A lowly tailor for Casanova named Pippo is forced to assume the role of his master; Beaucaire, a barber for the king, becomes the pretender of a champion swordsman who is a Duke. The premise of *Casanova's Big Night* seemed to be a refurbished version of the 1946 *Monsieur Beaucaire*—with a new location and some different humorous situations and a number of personality traits to allow Hope another channel for the exploitation of his talent.

The take-off on the reputation of Casanova shows the tight development by Hartmann and his cowriter Kanter. A man in a mask with the raiment of the famous lover and swordsman is attacked by three men with drawn blades and accused both of sexual advances on his wife by one of the assailants, and of not paying for the wine he took from his firm as a wine distiller. A flick of a sword and the mask comes off revealing it is not Casanova. As the tailor Pippo Popolino, Hope pleads for mercy and offers to compensate for the wine. "Oh, please spare my miserable life. I'll work off the debt. I'll make more wine for you. I've got big feet."

The wine merchant and his two companions leave Pippo because the encounter seems useless. Pippo resumes his disguise as Casanova in order to steal a kiss from Francesca, a maid (played by Joan Fontaine) that he has desired for a long time. She wants him to take off his mask before they kiss, but he insists "There's nothing underneath." This statement, plus many more, indicates some of the unconsciously comic faulty excuses used by Pippo. His identity is exposed by both Francesca and the real Casanova—played in a brief scene by an uncredited Vincent Price as the great lover and swordsman.

Many adventures develop for both Pippo and Francesca as they form an alliance and travel in Italy to escape the law. The plot escalates because the true Casanova has many debts and many trysts with women that backfire when a husband or father try to expose his lechery. Also, some of the foolish actions of Pippo make him a suspect as an impostor—which, of course, he is. In one scene authorities test him with an attractive courtesan. In a room without being observed, they kiss. Instead of the woman swooning under the embrace as it would happen with the great Casanova, Pippo collapses. Both the courtesan and the tailor confess in this room that both are frauds—that they were bragging about conquests to enhance their reputations. The liars are believed and Pippo goes free.

The attempt to embellish a popular sexually promiscuous legend of the upper-class in the society of the eighteenth century becomes a subject of the lampoon—almost to the point of satirical proportions. Some of same burlesque of salaciousness exists to a degree in Hope's earlier period costume picture, *Monsieur Beaucaire*, dealing with court intrigue during the time of Louis XV.

Eventually Pippo is caught and cast into prison. His cellmate happens to be Emo, with Lon Chaney, Jr. delivering a caricature of the serious role he had as the low I.Q. Lennie in the movie *Of Mice and Men* (1939), derived from the novelette by John Steinbeck. Emo, with childlike desires, wants to pet rabbits and mice. Changing clothes with the large, mentally defective person, Pippo ends up with a mouse in his pocket.

Without literary allusion, two scenes in the movie become replete with physical, comic actions that smack of slapstick. One is a sword fight with a champion and the other is Hope dressed as a dowager and Fontaine as a husband. In both actions there is an attempt to deceive the authorities who are pursuing Pippo and Francesca. The swordfight is not as innovative and as humorous as a similar duel with a master swordsman in *Monsieur Beaucaire*. In that film Beaucaire uses and hides behind musical instruments or a sheet music stand as he hacks away—not using elegant thrust and parries—trying to defend himself. As the Casanova impostor he exhibits similar lack of skill, but must maneuver near a hiding place so that she can knock the rival unconscious. Instead Pippo receives several blows, with one of them accidentally toppling him into his opponent so he wins the match by drawing first blood.

When Pippo and Francesca must appear in court before the king, they disguise themselves as high ranking visitors from a foreign country. As husband and wife their disguise is ludicrous, but the Italians believe they are from a weird land. The disguise came from the garb of the true baron and baroness from Cardovia who have been seized by Pippo and Francesca and pulled into a room where they can steal the dignitaries' dress.

When they emerged from the room, Francesca appeared dressed as a diminutive baron and Pippo as a large-bosomed baroness. Pippo tries to keep from revealing his deception by pulling the leader of the city-state, the Doge of Venice, onto the dance floor. He engages the reluctant Doge in a whirling dervish using a long scarf that sometimes hits the governor of a city in the face. Since Hope as the baroness is not supposed to know the language, he utters periodically the phrase "Farfa-Farfa-Pifick." His disguise continues to present trouble, the padded bosom of a dowager slipping down with the vigorous dancing and often sending him to the dance floor. The scene concludes with the Doge sending the pretender to jail and to the headsman's ax.

As the ax is about to decapitate Pippo, a freeze-fame device stops the last chop. A narrator declares that Bob "Orson Welles" Hope has a different ending. As he is about to die, Pippo seizes the ax and uses it to knock out or dispatch military guards around him He ducks as rapiers from a circle of men thrust home only to kill each other—forming a perfect wheel of dead bodies. Hope asks the audience if his version wasn't the desired one because it shows him as a hero and possesses a happy ending. Looking forward at the movie audience he discovers, to his disappointment, they do not support him and Paramount knew what the ending would be.

Of the three period adventure comedies, some of the best works in Hope's career—*The Princess and the Pirate, Monsieur Beaucaire,* and *Casanova's Big Night*—the latter picture could be ranked much higher than the earlier two. However, many of those who like the Hope pictures might favor *The Princess and the Pirate,* a well-mounted, colorful and action-jammed spectacle by MGM that has much to offer. This last period adventure movie actually took several cues from the *Pirate* and *Beaucaire.* I asked Ed Hartmann if he had been influenced by *Monsieur Beaucaire.* He said he didn't remember it and "didn't think there was any influence." To me, it appears Paramount saw the appeal of *The Princess and the Pirate* and tried to give some of the same colorful glitter and action to the Casanova picture that Hartmann and Kanter scripted for Hope.

Ed admired the vitality and indefatigable spirit of this sunny person.

"Bob came from vaudeville where he did five or six shows a day. So, I asked him how he kept up this tremendous, rigorous physical thing of the shows, the benefits—always on the go—the USO tours. He said, 'Well, years of vaudeville. This is nothing. This is relaxation.' So, he's the kind of guy I wouldn't see for ten years and I'll hear a voice saying, 'Hey, Ed!' I look over and I see it is Bob."

In our many interviews Ed let me know how grateful he was for the years he experienced with the comedian. After all, it was success for the Hope/Hartmann collaboration. Yes, many wonderful memories.

7
Of Songs, Music Men, and Hartmann

"I know Jay and Ray well and could tell you a great deal about them," Ed reminisced. He had kept up with his friendship with them over decades. "Their songs were nominated many times by the Academy. "'Buttons and Bows' for my *The Paleface* won an Oscar. Also won for 'Mona Lisa' [created for the 1950 *Captain Carey USA*] and 'Que Sera Sera.' That was for Hitchcock's *The Man Who Knew Too Much* [1956]. I tried to get them for my two productions starring Olsen and Johnson, but Universal had contracted musicians so I couldn't use them."

In an April 19, 2001 interview Hartmann referred to Jay Livingston and Ray Evans, two of the most prolific tunesmiths who were so talented in their field they could not only create hit songs for movies but could score the total picture. The music men would make a significant contribution to the next to last of the seven films Ed penned for Bob Hope, *Here Come the Girls*.

After I viewed this sixth movie in his long-term link with the comedian, I asked Ed if this work wasn't more of a musical than any other that he wrote for the actor. "I was told this was the best Hope picture I did," he explained. The screenwriter created the original story and cowrote the motion picture with Hal Kanter. "You mean *Here Come the Girls* wasn't designed to be a musical?" I quizzed him. With an uncharacteristic use of an expletive he said, "They fucked up." The very proper gentleman from St. Louis obviously was disgusted with the final results. Ed thought the use of a male actor who was noted for his crooning brought more songs into the picture than needed. His excellent memory failed him because he obviously had to be told the lead's name was Tony Martin. Naturally, something he wished to forget. And his view proved to be correct, since some of Martin's songs were cut from the final release.

Hartmann's basic story for the lead comedian can be revealed by Hope's character, Stanley Snodgrass, who bemoans his fate when he is fired from a stage show, "I'm the oldest living chorus boy. Failing is the only thing I've been a success at." The premise seems very fruitful for a comedy character extension of Hope's best work. Snodgrass's self-analysis shows a new dimension that provides sympathy not often realized in the comedian's portraits. To complicate this situation a madman threatens the leading man (Tony Martin's role) because the killer wishes the leading lady (Arlene Dahl's role) to turn her affections in his directions. Snodgrass becomes a substitute target as bait to catch the potential murderer. The fall guy thereby gets unbridled flattery from the producer and the leads to keep him in the show—even though his performance results in many mistakes and even clumsy falls. Not aware of his inept portrayal of a leading man, Sidney becomes inflated with the compliments he receives. In the climactic scene he realizes he is the target of the killer who throws knives at Snodgrass while he is on stage struggling to escape death. The humor of the comedian as a coward who hides behind people and stage set pieces gives Hope a chance to show how he can execute risible physical actions.

Since there are eleven musical portions of *Here Come the Girls,* songwriters Jay Livingston and Ray Evans provide significant contributions to this comic genre—to the point the film can be classified as a musical. One of the best numbers, "You Got Class," is executed as a duet by Bob Hope and Rosemary Clooney. The comedian reaches back to his earlier profession as a dancer and handles this song and several others with considerable skill. Newcomer Clooney fulfills a most promising talent in her vocalization of "You Got Class" as she urges "the oldest chorus boy" to realize he has the ability to succeed. She also develops the lyric song, "When You Love Someone."

But Ms. Clooney does not contribute much as a costar for Hope. She will achieve stage presence in her future work for the big screen medium and in her television show in the late '50s. Also, the acting and singing of Tony Martin and Arlene Dahl remain only passable in this film drama. In short, Hope shines, but he has very little support. Hartmann's evaluation of his last work for Hope is right. *Here Come the Girls* should have been focused as a comedy with a few musical elements. In the early script version by Ed and Hal Kanter, producer Don Hartman praised them for the creation of "the best Bob Hope comedy ever written." Ironically, the results became merely a good Hope movie.

One of Ed's earliest associations with the musical, *Time Out for Rhythm,* now proves to be one of the best of this popular genre of the year 1941. While the sparkle of dancer-singer Ann Miller contributes much to this film, the total movie holds up much better than so many of this type. There is a dual plot that gives some variation to the story often used with a musical. One portion focuses on the discovery of a talented person, another the perfection of a nightclub singer. The merging of these two plots occurs when an elaborate variety show is created. Two women provide the leads with one specializing in her dance skills, the other her singing talent. Prominent radio star singer of the early '30s Rudy Vallee becomes a talent scout with Richard Lane when he advises Rosemary Lane how to sing a ballad. Rudy and Richard become cotalent agents and when a maid with considerable dancing skills is discovered, a quartet of expertise for variety shows or musicals is generated. The two men are singers. A movie comedian, Allen Jenkins, provides his talent at the piano, dancing, and many humorous touches for a fifth part in the picture. With more limited success, Columbia Pictures added periodic skits by the studio's two-reel comic team, the Three Stooges. The main actors do more to help sell the work during a period when audiences received a flood of this genre.

Songwriter Sammy Cahn and musical score composer Saul Chaplin make a significant contribution to *Time Out for Rhythm* with a variety of songs: "Time Out for Rhythm," "Boogie-woogie Man," "As If You Didn't Know," and "Obviously the Gentleman Prefers to Dance." Cahn was not nominated for his tunes in this picture but he would soon be nominated about thirty times for a Best Song Academy Award, with four wins. He would give Frank Sinatra some of his hit songs such as "High Hopes," "The Second Time Around," and "My Kind of Town." Saul Chaplin would eventually win Best Score Oscars for *An American in Paris* (1951), *Seven Brides for Seven Brothers* (1954), and *West Side Story* (1951).

Another musical Hartmann developed for Columbia came out the same year as *Time Out for Rhythm*, 1941. *Sweetheart of the Campus* becomes more important for the talent rather than the quality of the musical numbers. Ruby Keeler (noted for her tap dancing in such '30s musicals as *42nd Street*) makes her last starring film appearance. As her career waned, two important leads, Ozzie Nelson with his orchestra and his wife Harriet Hilliard, become an essential part of the total plot. This pair would have a brief career in '40s films, but would become radio and television stars with their sitcom *Ozzie and Harriet* for two decades, from 1944 to 1966.

The working title for this '40s musical indicates the attempt to exploit Keeler's background as a star dancer of the '30s, *Betty Co-Ed, Sweetheart of the Campus*. As the featured dancer in a nightclub near an all-male college she is considered "the sweetheart," and she becomes the Miss Fixit by recruiting men and eventually women to correct the sagging enrollment of the institution called Lambert College. Of course, the efforts of Ozzie and Harriet with their talent in developing radio and television shows to promote the college almost makes them Mr. and Mrs. Fixit in the plot of the picture. The husband and wife's use of the media now appears prophetic. Television also became important in the plot of *Time Out for Rhythm*, both released in June 1941. This was the infancy of the medium that obviously fascinated screenwriter Edmund Hartmann, and this also might be considered prophetic, since he would become an important writer and producer of sitcoms *My Three Sons* and *Family Affair*.

A Paramount 1942 musical, *True to the Army*, had an elaborate source history. Originally a novel by Edward Hope called *She Loves Me Not*, it was adapted to the stage by playwright Howard Lindsay. Then Paramount released a movie using the original title in 1934 starring Bing Crosby and Miriam Hopkins. Paramount assigned Ed Hartmann and Val Burton to redo the picture and they updated the story to include a wartime theme. The first film version centered on a college plot. Hopkins is a witness to a gangland murder and she seeks refuge with Princeton male students by assuming a disguise as a young man. The switch in the '40s film has Judy Canova disguised as a male recruit in the army under similar pursuit by a gang's attempt to kill a female witness to a murder.

The updated, revised *True to the Army* does profit from strong acting from comedian actors such as Jerry Colonna, William Demarest, and, of course, Judy Canova. Romantic leads Allan Jones and Ann Miller also make substantial contributions.

Born in the south, Judy came naturally to an act as a cornpone comedienne in vaudeville and radio. She had a jaunty air with a likeable naïveté. She is paired with the eccentric comedian Jerry Colonna who has bulging eyes and an oversize handlebar mustache. With a wacko persona, he always portrayed an inept person whose sanity is suspect. On the other hand, William Demarest enacts a relatively normal comic character, Sergeant Butes, who has trouble handling his position of authority because he is naïve and easily conned. Allen Jones has a few moments of light comedy but he is used mostly as a stage director who develops shows to entertain the troops.

Judy Canova as hillbilly Daisy disguised as a young man—almost like a boy—proves to be a sharpshooter when engaged in practice on the army's rifle range. In the climactic army show scene, the gangsters try to shoot Daisy, but she has a gun for a sharp-shooting act on stage. She outshoots them in the theatre and the police capture the gang.

Comedienne Canova employs a technique of humor used by other singers of the '40s and '50s. Joan Davis and Betty Hutton, for example, would deliver a straight version of a song and switch into a burlesque rendering of the tune. Judy sings a sweet version of "I Can't Give You Anything but Love" and suddenly breaks into a pseudo-opera run of high notes, a short jazz rendition, and a hillbilly version accompanied by yodeling. As a soldier in the army she goes with comrades to a nightclub and gets drunk. A woman takes a liking to her, thinking she is a man, and dances with her. Judy shows her skill as a comic dancer as she gets tossed around in a jitterbug number.

There are seven musical portions in *True to the Army*. The seventh is a production featuring Allan Jones singing the title song. He sings several numbers by one of the great composers of the American theatre, Frank Loesser. For this film he is credited with the lyrics for "Spangles on My Tights," "Wacky for Khaki," "Jitterbug Lullaby," and "Need I Speak." Loesser wrote many songs for films that became popular, however he is probably best known for such Broadway musicals as *Guys and Dolls, The Most Happy Fella,* and *How to Succeed in Business Without Really Trying.*

With a wide variety of talents, effective songs, and production numbers, *True to the Army* and *Time Out for Rhythm* are the two best musicals Hartmann helped to create in the '40s.

Ed had some association with three other musicals or variety shows *Ma, He's Making Eyes at Me* (1940), *Rhythm of the Islands* (1943), and *Variety Girl* (1947). The screenwriter-producer had only a sketchy memory of his role in the creation of these mediocre works. Bosley Crother, never a celebrator of lighter cinema fare, wrote in the *New York Times:*

> This is the season for fashion shows, and that is about all you get in "Ma! He's Making Eyes at Me": now double-billed at the palace with "Virginia City." Outside of it, you also get a cut-rate, bargain-basement story about a press agent who builds up a beautiful model as Miss Manhattan in order to sell a

cheap line of goods, arranges a stunt marriage for her and then marries her himself. It is a limp and foolish little picture, inexcusable on any other grounds than as a chaser to follow the main feature.

The title, incidentally, has nothing to do with it, except that Constance Moore sings that song.

Of course, *Ma, He's Making Eyes at Me* does have a few features that make it on a par with many musicals or variety shows of the decade. Ed Sullivan, a newspaperman who graduated to be the stiffest TV master of ceremonies, developed the story. The fact that the film provided a lead-in for the Western, *Virginia City*, (a follow-up picture prompted by the popular 1939 *Dodge City*), automatically put the film in dim light for any critic. Also, *Virginia City* had some of the big Warner stars of the Western predecessor. In the 1940 movie, Errol Flynn repeats his hero role with the assistance of Miriam Hopkins, Randolph Scott, Humphrey Bogart, and Alan Hale. With more modest budget and casting, Tom Brown, Constance Moore, and Peggy Chamberlain do, at least, workmanship jobs of making *Ma, He's Making Eyes at Me* entertaining.

With his close relationship with certain actors in the many movies he scripted, Hartmann remembered such character actors as Andy Devine. However, the 1943 *Rhythm of the Islands* would hardly spark recall. He and two other writers were credited with the label "additional dialogue." I indicated to Ed that in my thirty years plus of educational and community theatre I had to strain the brain to recall specific projects and I didn't engage in the whirlwind activity of a Hollywood screenwriter. Of a number of films he was associated with he would remark, "I don't remember a thing about it." *Rhythm of the Islands* evidently was one of those films that would not stimulate recall. He, of course, remembered the leads from other pictures. The three leads, Allan Jones, Jane Frazee, and Andy Devine were important players in other works of the period. Universal sponsored a typical escapist creation of the wartime period. Five songs and specialty numbers are woven into a plot that has Jones and Devine trying to sell island real estate to a millionaire tourist played by Ernest Truex. While the pair have a shady deal going, the affection Jones develops for the wealthy man's daughter brings about his reformation and he then handles the deal on a straight basis. While this picture presents a hodgepodge of cliché elements—especially the songs and production number dances, it satisfied the public's fascination with Hawaiian music. Also, the romantic scenes starring Allan Jones and Jane Frazee had two competent singers who could act so much better than the average vocalists. A sprinkle of comedy throughout the film by another duo provided the audience with the variety the '40s audiences found appealing. The pair, Andy Devine and Mary Wickes, enacted the roles of struggling lovers. Devine, pursued by an attractive daughter of a native chief, is cowed by a domineering Wickes who becomes a verbal and physical match with anyone who gets in the way of "her man." Ms. Wickes joined the many aggressive females, such as Martha Raye, Joan Davis, and Betty Hutton, who became crowd-pleasing comediennes in the '40s.

While *Rhythm of the Islands* has a plot of sorts, the 1947 *Variety Girl* may be an example of too many cooks dissipating the creative effort. This was typical of a studio's development of a picture to show off their contract players. The two studios with such a variety and amount of talented actors were MGM and Paramount. And, the heads of these two movie companies wanted such amalgamation of talents. So, the variety show in the '40s and '50s produced an audience reaction of "Oh, look. That's Alan Ladd singing. I didn't know he could." Or, "Who is that?"

And, Alan Ladd does sing. He has Dorothy Lamour to assist him as they handle one of the best songs of the picture, "Tallahassee," by Frank Loesser, one of Paramount's best composers, who contributes a total of seven songs.

The star of *Variety Girl*, Mary Hatcher, came from the stage as an effective singer in *Oklahoma!* However, her promising beginning had a career that consisted of seven movies. Another young performer, Olga San Juan, played a similar starring role and had a similar limited stint in films. The third lead in this plot on which was pasted a number of skits and songs seemed also to be cursed by fate. Actually, Paramount didn't know how to handle DeForest Kelly, who played a talent scout and provided a romantic attachment for Mary Hatcher. From this important role as a leading man, Kelly soon became cast in secondary or minor roles. His career would move from near oblivion to stardom when producer Gene Roddenberry gave him several parts in television, especially a role in a failed television series *333 Montgomery*. When he assumed the role of Dr. Leonard "Bones" McCoy for the popular television series, *Star Trek,* it provided him a comeback in 1966, nineteen years after his lead in *Variety Girl.*

Miss Hatcher proved to be an effective actress and singer in this film directed by George Marshall. She handled the dialogue for her character Catherine Brown who supposedly was a naïve young girl struggling to make her career in the movies. She fit the part of a young, spirited woman, the role of an ingenue. And her singing indicated she had the stylistic range from jazz to semi-operatic variations. She is especially effective in her rendition of a Loesser song, "He Can Waltz."

While they were slightly involved with the plot by being present on the Paramount lot, Bob Hope and Bing Crosby were headliners. They sang and danced to the tune, "Harmony." Hope took over for a stage show as master of ceremonies for the conclusion of *Variety Girl*. The total impact of this picture fades with time since many people who would view this work today would not be acquainted with even the stars who appear briefly throughout the film.

If the musical elements of the comedy, variety, and musical genres Edmund Hartmann scripted are examined, the skills of the composers can be seen to be the solid contribution. Frank Loesser's work becomes important and when it comes to the Hope comedies Jay Livingston and Ray Evans become the masters. Even the Hope movie Ed thinks didn't go the way it should have, *Here Come the Girls*, has the intriguing "You Got Class," and, of course, there were the award winning "Silver Bells" from *The Lemon Drop Kid* and "Buttons and Bows" from *The Paleface.*

"When I was at Universal I had an idea for a musical," Ed told me after I had read him a formative version of the chapter on this genre. He set forth one of his disappointing experiences by reminiscing: "At college I used to write the book, music, and lyrics. I suggested to the head of the studio that I do the book music, and lyrics for a little musical picture. And he thought it was a very good idea and liked the picture and assigned me to write the total film. The producer was William Sistrem. Well, I was working on it—writing the whole thing—when a friend of mine from New York, Oscar Hammerstein, came to Hollywood and we had lunch together. He asked me what I was doing and I told him I was writing the book, music, and lyrics of a movie. He told me 'They will never let you do it. It will be your picture instead of their picture.' He was exactly right. As I got into the film, they paid less and less attention to it. They finally assigned me to something else. Nobody had read what I had written."

It was one of his greatest disheartening occurrences in a Hollywood that too often bound and gagged its writers.

8
Bound and Gagged: The Censored and Damned

"Even my mother asked me if I were a Communist," Hartmann told me, because he became enmeshed in the age of Hollywood blacklisting.

Ronald Reagan, according to Ed, became a snitch. It was the age of paranoia as if there were a Red under every bed. The national government became engaged in witch trials with a very persistent House Un-American Activities Committee. It was the beginning of his metamorphosis into Hollywood's arch-conservative politics. Reagan once was a liberal Democrat and the head of the Actors Guild. However, he saw the ominous "writing on the wall" that would reverse his views. Marsha Hunt, an actress who had important roles in the films until she was blacklisted for her progressive (not communistic) views, recalled what some thought were Reagan's broad-minded views before he became converted to a right-wing stand. He mouthed liberal ideology, Hunt remembered, until he ended up a bore.

In the late '40s and early '50s the United States witnessed an inquisition directed at Hollywood because it was thought that the industry had filmmakers, especially screenwriters and actors, who were traitors. Presumably these creators were engaged in creating dramas that used Communistic propaganda. Under extreme pressure from an establishment that switched from hating the "Nazis" to hating the "Commies," the nation focused on a political ideology that some believed would "destroy the American way of life." A code emerged that held it morally valid to incriminate friends. Ed recalled that he walked down Sunset Boulevard with a fellow screenwriter when two other writers passed by. "Hello, Ed." Both greeted Hartmann while ignoring Ed's companion. Ed indicated that the snub was tied to the paranoia of the times when his colleague remarked, "Those used to be my two best friends."

Ed continued, recalling the actions of the informer who would be elected to the highest office in the land. He was pushed to this position because he became the darling of those with a far right political persuasion.

"Ronald Reagan would listen to those who spoke at meetings and if he thought a speaker expressed ideas that were not acceptable he would report them to the FBI," Ed told me. There were other actor informers such as Adolphe Menjou, Sterling Hayden, Robert Taylor, Ward Bond, and Robert Montgomery. Many people in Hollywood had their careers on the line. Consequently a person might believe it to be a patriotic duty to name names of suspected communist sympathizer—even if it might give the informer a label of Judas.

Ronald Reagan, as head of the Actors Guild had the responsibility of supporting the members. However, he refused to back such actors as Charles Chaplin, Jeff Corey, Howard Da Silva, John Garfield, Canada Lee, John Randolph, Paul Robeson, and Gale Sondergaard. Most of these actors may have had liberal leanings in their views or had become disenchanted with any organization that might have some link to socialistic philosophy.

With a retrospective of today, it appears that the movement toward thought control was more directed at liberal ideas since communism had little influence in the United States. The country struggled through the deep depression of the '30s and an internal takeover by a foreign power only existed in the imagination of the red-baiters who had to have someone to hate—often for political or economic advantage. Unfortunately, the studios easily became a part of the movement to purge its creative talents when those talents did not embrace conservative ideas.

Hartmann gave two anecdotes to show some executive compliance with the witch-hunt of the Congress. According to Ed, writer-producer Dore Schary, known for significant message pictures and thereby his liberal views, had to bow to the wishes of the studios and announce to writers that if they wanted to remain in the business they could not have Communist connections. Fear of banishment may have prompted the hypocrisy Ed witnessed while eating at the commissary. In the other end of the room he heard a sudden cheering of a group who witnessed the entrance of some dignitary. To Ed's surprise, after standing on a chair, he saw that all the supposed acclaim was for the most infamous red-baiter of all investigators, Senator Joseph McCarthy.

One of the most curious features of this Hollywood inquisition became a form of doublethink, which George Orwell developed in his novel *1984*, a work created in 1949. This dystopia appeared as the film capital of the United States experienced its hell on earth. The establishment tried to put forth the view that no blacklist existed. Victor Navasky in his *Naming Names* noted, "The Motion Picture Association of America denied that the industry kept a blacklist, but it said that no Fifth Amendment takers (or First Amendment takers either, for that matter) who hadn't purged themselves before an appropriate congressional committee could work in Hollywood" (pp. 86-87). In his insightful expose Navasky reveals that Screen Actor Guild head Ronald Reagan touted the company line by saying, "We will not be a party to a blacklist" (p. 87). However, this organization banned actors who had past Communistic connections from membership in the Guild and even uncooperative witnesses who appeared before the Congressional Committee.

Ed Hartmann indicated his disenchantment with a Hollywood politically divided—split into a dichotomy. "Both sides became extremists," he said. And he agreed with me in an interview that one of the most maligned writers who received the industry's scarlet letter was Dalton Trumbo, who spent thirteen years in a blacklisted limbo. Under the pseudonym of Robert Rich he wrote the screenplay for *The Brave One* in 1956—finally awarded an Oscar in 1975 by the Academy for this film. "I knew Dalton well," Edmund said. "He told me he was not a Communist—that he was a pacifist." A widely reported statement by Trumbo paralleled the view that Hartmann expressed in this interview: "We were all victims." That even meant the informers. They often received a black pall of hate from colleagues who once liked them.

During the start of World War II the United States began to develop an alliance with Russia. Some writers lauded the courageous stand of that country against Germany before we entered the war. Richard Collins and Paul Jarrico penned a pro-Russian movie, *The Song of Russia* (1943). While Jerrico refused to name names before the House Un-American Activities Committee, Collins became what some of his writer colleagues called "a turncoat." While he became a key informer on fellow filmmakers, a hack writer Martin Berkeley admitted he was a card-carrying Communist for seven years. He satisfied the investigators by naming over one hundred workers in the industry who he claimed were fellow travelers or, using the dreaded term of the day, "Reds."

The cost to the informer writers was twofold; they were snubbed by their colleagues and seldom recovered with an outstanding credit for their screenwriting. Leo Townsend and Martin Berkeley were two examples of fading careers. The blacklisting became a two-way street—both the informer and the person with the mark of Cain became victims.

Hartmann related how he became incensed by another version of a blacklist. It was Hollywood's censorship and damning of a race—the blacks in the industry. They were allowed as entertainers—as song and dance talents and often as the comic relief in sentimental, humorous pieces. Two male actors, Paul Robeson and Canada Lee appeared in serious films: Robeson in *The Emperor Jones* (1933), an adapted Eugene O'Neill play, and Lee in director Alfred Hitchcock's *Lifeboat* (1944). Both were extremely talented stage and film actors, but they were lured by liberal and communistic philosophies that promised civil rights for their race. Both found themselves unable to obtain roles in film.

Regarding the industry's "blackness" problem, Edmund related one of the most absurd concerns of studio heads not to offend Southern U.S. box office sensitivities. As producer-writer of one of the best Abbott and Costello movies, *The Naughty Nineties,* Ed said he was pleased that studio heads wanted to view the filming of a musical piece featuring a male blackface chorus. As part of a riverboat show, it reflected the type of entertainment of the past. To his disappointment, he began to realize the observation was not to praise the efforts of all engaged in the scene. The executives wanted to be sure the blacks (whites with burnt cork on their face) would not mix with the whites. Southern sensitivities and a possible box office ban in this region of the United States might be the result with the inclusion of this sequence in the movie. It was perplexing for the writer-producer for this 1945 show. How much had Al Jolson and Eddie Cantor made capital with their blackface song routines on both stage and screen?

Segregation in the restaurant, hotel, and swimming pool evidently needed to be applied to the fictional world of the film drama. Hartmann discovered Nat King Cole with his trio doing a nightclub act and wanted to use his group in his Olsen and Johnson production of *See My Lawyer*. Again, separation seemed to be necessary in the '40s decade. Ed had the group do their song dressed as cooks and on an elevated stage on wheels. Thereby, Cole's brief turn for the film became properly severed and segregated from the white folks This was especially important when white women dancers were to appear clearly separated from blacks.

And in his *Naughty Nineties* Ed had an ingénue from below the Mason-Dixon Line who thought blacks couldn't possibly achieve her I.Q. "I see you have some of them in our picture?" she queried. "Can they learn their lines?" "Yes," Ed assured her. "Isn't that wonderful," she said. From her patronizing reply it seemed obvious that her genteel world of learned racial bias probably had little chance of being penetrated.

Few members of the studio conceived or desired a change in attitude toward the black, negra, Negro, nigger, or even the strange term "coon." Today the label "African American" seems to be preferred much like the politically correct "Native American." But in the '40s there was a great deal of direct racial prejudice

There was a bootblack from Kansas on the studio grounds who had the education to be in a much higher status job. Ed found out that he graduated from Wichita University, an institution that had a sports program in the same conference as Hartmann's Washington University in Saint Louis. To Ed he spoke the king's English like the college man he was. However, a black in this profession had to play the game. When a customer arrived for a shoeshine he lapsed into the expected stereotype: "Ah'll gonna give ya the best shine ya ebber had."

Asked why he, Hartmann, had troubles writing for director George Marshall, part of the scriptwriter's distaste for his film colleague came down to his prejudice. He recalled a comment, "If I enter a ballpark with 50,000 and there is one nigger there, I can smell him."

This racially disparaging remark did not get picked up by the genteel press media of that age. Today, such a remark would hit the papers and be broadcast on radio and television by a media that has almost embraced the scandal of the tabloid press. The author of this view would soon be out of a position— ironically, today's version of blacklisting.

We sometimes think all of the irrational suspicion and even hatred of a race, a religion, and a political system has diminished. The Latino and black races believe the motion picture and television media ignore them. Those in charge of the content believe there is not enough of an audience for serious dramatic themes focusing on minorities to hire writers and actors of ethnic minorities or of minority races. In spite of the progress that has been made, the same rationale of the past is still present. Prominent television commentators such as Bob Novak and George Will still seem to be fighting the Cold War with Russia. Any criticism of our capitalistic system, even when there is valid evidence of a fault, produces the still dreaded term "socialism" or "communism." And, of course, such a conservative front will not produce media dramas critical of our system of government.

Even more direct in its bias is an Internet essay from *MediaLink* from the Ayn Rand Institute, a group that presents irrational political diatribes. This relates to the Hollywood investigations of the '40s and '50s. Michael S. Berliner, a Ph.D., writes "By joining the Party (an undisputed fact), the filmmakers were not merely making an ideological statement but were agreeing to take orders to commit actions—criminal and treasonable actions, since the Party, and the Soviet government is served, which was openly dedicated to the overthrow of the U.S. government." Of course, this could be questioned since the overthrow of our system could hardly be a motive. As actor Melvyn Douglas commented years after the House Un-American Activities Committee investigation of the Communist, the accusations remained invalid. The Communists became followers of the liberals and not vice versa. Liberalism, not Communism, may, in fact, have been the true target. And, there is a possible interpretation that members of the studio establishment never were fond of the Guilds and wanted to mute the power of these unions.

Edmund Hartmann would prove his effective leadership when he became head of the Writers Guild. Ed told me he adhered to a moderate course in his view of a censorship that could be conquered with time—especially when a nation began to see the harm visited on highly talented filmmakers. It became obvious that many times such writers and actors were banned because they did not embrace reactionary political views.

Ed's view on Hollywood's racial bigotry indicated he became a liberal when producers relegated blacks to song and dance plus comic roles. However, he developed an objective and temperate position during the blacklisting period. While he agreed with me that actors and writers were not afforded due process in the investigations, he witnessed many of these filmmakers engaging in tirades. The battle polarized both groups. Neither the conservatives nor the liberals were reasonable in their rigid concepts and stands. Times would change and the censored and damned, the blacklisted and the blacks, would achieve a rightful status in the industry.

9
Much Ado about Family on TV

While it has not been fully realized, the blacklisting of talent in the media, film, radio, and television, lasted just over two decades. Hartman told me that even in the 1960s he had to call a number to clear a potential writer for the CBS television series, *My Three Sons*. A phantom on the other end of the line would tell him if it were feasible to hire the person. Ed told me, "I just had a phone number to call. I didn't know who I was talking to." While he was a writer-producer for this long-running, twelve-year situation comedy, his busy schedule placed a demand on him to hire other writers. Despite this unwanted intrusion employing an outmoded kind of censorship, Hartmann had a successful career in the television medium.

Before he assumed the command post as producer and writer of four situation comedies, Ed as early as the '50s dabbled to the point of making a significant penetration into the electronic medium of the small screen. One of his best efforts saw fruition with what was called a "book" musical for NBC's *The Colgate Comedy Hour*. He adapted a television version of Cole Porter's 1941 stage musical, *Let's Face It*. This high profile, lavish program by NBC had launched an earlier Cole Porter stage musical adaptation on February 28, 1954, *Anything Goes*. This refurbished and minimized version featured Ethel Merman, Frank Sinatra, and Bert Lahr. Comedian Lahr would later be hired for Hartmann's one hour adaptation of *Let's Face It*, with a television broadcast on November 21, 1954. However, the actor expressed concern with the part that he was assigned. For Hartmann's version, Bert Lahr got a chance to play two roles, that of Frankie Burns and, in comic drag, Aunt Pamela Burns.

"I rewrote and extended his role," Ed remembered. If it would appear that Hartmann and the producers were playing loose with the original stage musical so that Cole Porter's version faded, it should be realized much tinkering with the theatre work also happened in 1941. Danny Kaye enacted the leading role of Jerry Walker and this comedian's wife and songwriter, Sylvia Fine, added to the

Porter songs that fit Kaye's patter song talent. The condensed 1954 TV version of *Let's Face It* not only eliminates such Kaye-type songs to fit lead singer-dancer Gene Nelson's skills, it also adds songs from other Porter stage musicals—such as "It's De-lovely" from the 1936 *Red, Hot and Blue*. Another added tune to the TV version of *Let's Face It*, "I've Got You under My Skin," turned out to be a revived creation from one of Porter's brief ventures in writing for Hollywood musicals. Cole had written this hit song for MGM's 1936 *Born to Dance*.

When he became a writer-producer for CBS, Ed wrote some television scripts for actress Eve Arden. Before he took over for a series called *The Eve Arden Show*, the actress held the lead role of an assertive teacher in the situation comedy series *Our Miss Brooks* in 127 episodes from October 3, 1952 to September 21, 1956. For her series that began September 17, 1957 Hartmann told me, "I wrote some of her scripts as I produced the show. She didn't want to do broad comedy." A description of *The Eve Arden Show* indicates that it was a more sophisticated role than she had previously depicted:

> This comedy series cast the actress as novelist Liza Hammond. Liza supplemented her writing income by giving lectures. . . . While Liza was out lecturing the population, her mother, Nora, was at home looking after her 12-year-old twin daughters, Jenny and Mary. This series was based on the autobiography of the writer Emily Kimbrough. (*The Complete Directory to Prime Time Network and Cable TV Shows: 1945-Present,* edited by Tim Brooks and Earle Marsh, pp. 319-320.)

Obviously, this plot shows Hartmann developing his future success as a writer-producer of family situation comedy. His formative launching into this genre did not bring the recognition he desired. His *Eve Arden Show* lasted for only 26 episodes, from September 17, 1957 to March 25, 1958.

However, his handling of the situation comedy, *My Three Sons,* brought him to the peak of his career for CBS because it became the long running hit of his television years. This series lasted twelve years, from 1960 to 1972—bested only two years more by another family sitcom, *The Adventures of Ozzie and Harriet.* The reason for *My Three Sons'* long run became evident when I examined some of the 369 shows.

First of all, the writing of each presentation remains superior to most television situation comedies of the '60s. As a writer and producer Hartmann supervised the creation of each script. "It became necessary to have someone to know what characters and plot situations existed in previous shows," Ed recalled about his producer role. He also supervised the crafting of each installment. As a result, the plots remained tight and logical from the beginning to the conclusion of each show. Occasionally some of the denouements involving a mistaken identity or situation seem forced. However, this is standard for so many American situation comedies. A great deal of emphasis is placed on wrapping up comic threads without leaving any incident hanging. Anyone familiar with British sitcoms may remember that such works as *Fawlty Towers* do not always resolve a conflict between husband and wife.

Second of all, the drawing of the characters allowed for a wide variety and an effective amount of humor. Each of the leading characters has different comic facets. And five characters provide this range of humor: the father (Steve Douglas), the oldest son (Mike), the middle son (Robbie), and the youngest (Chip) plus the caretakers of the house for the busy father (Grandpa "Bub" and later Uncle Charley).

The persona of *My Three Sons* reveals a close relationship to the subgenre of comedy tied to genteel humor. It evolved from the sentimental tradition of British drama of the eighteenth century with some links to the sophisticated comedy of the previous century. However, the series supervised by Edmund Hartmann always avoided the maudlin touches of a predecessor, *Father Knows Best*. This TV series ran for about ten years (October 3, 1953 to April 5, 1963) and emphasized a fictional ideal family that employed a sentimental wholesomeness that existed in some fantasyland. For example, Robert Young as father Jim Anderson resolved some misalliance conflict that his daughter became involved in with another girl. The father delivered a lecture on her self-serving attitude. Father Steve Douglas, as played by Fred MacMurray, sometimes gave advice to one of his sons, but it evolved in a commonsense way without the saccharine tone of the sentimental comedy, *Father Knows Best*. No Anderson offspring would doubt the motives of their father; however, the sons of Steve sometimes found their father old-fashioned, and other times not acting his age, such as when he took a liking to a nightclub singer that they thought had a checkered past. In short, humor in Ed's sitcom built situations and character development on more realistic bases.

Caretakers and cooks for the Douglas household, Grandpa Bub O'Casey and Uncle Charley O'Casey offer a counterpoint to situations that stop just short of the sentimental. Both are curmudgeons from a world outside the neat world of suburbia. Bub comes from the vaudeville stage and Charley lived the colorful life as a sailor. Consequently, Bub applies the experiences of the theatre to the struggles of the three sons with peers and girlfriends. Charley, likewise, adds the salty background of his world to the sons and their father. These two characters assist the writers and producer to give the audience a type of humor that lends spice to the genteel mode of comedy.

And what developed as the risible nature of the boys' character and lives, the three sons? Variety exists even here while the humor cuts close to the sentimental path. The eldest, Mike, takes many situations too seriously—to the point he ends up looking foolish. Robbie, the son in the middle, floats in a universe of relativity, often undercutting Mike's rigid views. Chip, of course, lives in the domain of childhood, looking at each incident from his own perspective. As a result the sons cross-purpose of views sometimes produces comedy.

Not all of these various attitudes of the characters in *My Three Sons* come into play with each episode. And that is part of the charm of the series. Even the humor produced by the shaggy dog, Tramp, evolves in some sequences. The dog, who predates the antics of the plucky humanlike reactions of Eddie, the Jack Russell hound on the sitcom *Frazier*, has programs with his predominance in the title: "Tramp—the Hero," (October 26, 1961), "It's a Dog's Life," (March 18, 1965), and "Tramp and the Prince" (April 15, 1965).

Third of all, audiences seemed to love the year by year maturing process of the family. The two older sons experienced love affairs that usually developed into comic entanglements. Chip, played by Stanley Livingston, went from a child to a boy in his teens. Audiences followed the changes as new complications in the lives of the boys—revealed them growing into men. The writers and producer Hartmann therefore had a chance to keep the comic situations fresh and interesting.

Fourth of all, the casting of *My Three Sons* had the distinct advantage of such extensively experienced actors as Fred MacMurray, William Frawley, and William Demarest in the adult roles. Even the roles of the sons came to the show with credits. Tim Considine (Mike) acted with MacMurray in Disney's *The Shaggy Dog* (1959). Don Grady (Robbie) appeared as a mouseketeer on the *Mickey Mouse Club*. The youngest son, Chip, played by Stanley Livingston had credits on *The Adventures of Ozzie and Harriet*. Consequently, the producer, directors, and writers of *My Three Sons* had a much easier task of creating this long-running series.

While it is impossible to pick one or two *My Three Sons* programs that are typical, a brief summary and analysis of two works might give some indication of the nature and quality of the series.

The examples are "Tramp and the Prince" (April 15, 1965) and "Monsters and Junk Like That" (November 5, 1965). This first show employs a switch from the usual comic plot of mistaken identity from human to animal. Tramp, the longhaired mutt of the Douglas family, runs away chasing a cat and is lost. Chip and Ernie, the youngest members of the family, mistake an identical stray, Prince, for the Douglas dog. However, Prince is the pet of a dowager whose chauffeur picks up Tramp. Since both creatures exhibit contrary characteristics, (Tramp is laid back and Prince is manic), the owners check out their pets at the same vet and there is a reconciliation with the proper master.

"Monsters and Junk Like That" focused on the comic talents of Fred MacMurray as he tried to help son Ernie in a school play that the boy had fashioned for a class project. Fred had to dress in armor that looked much like the Tin Woodman in *The Wizard of Oz*. As this character Steve Douglas, the actor executes the comedy of frustration and embarrassment. His monster dress proves to be too tight and he can't get out of it. He attempts to get to his son's school via a car and can't bend enough to get in the driver's side: An attempt to ride one of his boys' bikes also is futile because he can't get on this conveyance. He walks. Of course, awkwardly. The visor of the armor falls down and he eventually falls on his back. People ignore him, but he eventually gets to the school and helps his son with the performance.

These are only sketchy examples of the long-running *My Three Sons*, which Ed became involved in during its third season. The favorable response of this series prompted Hartmann to launch his own creation, *Family Affair*, a sitcom that had a television life of 138 episodes—from 1966 to 1971. Some similarities with *My Three Sons* indicated that the concept developed by Ed followed a popular formula. The head of an adopted family, Uncle Bill Davis, became a surrogate father when his brother and sister-in-law are killed in an automobile accident. Bill, played by Brian Keith, is a highly successful, busy president of a construction company and needs a caretaker for the house and family. Nigel French, enacted by the British character actor Sebastian Cabot, has many facets of the earlier sitcom male fixer for the family—therefore, the series becomes shades of *My Three Sons*—of course. And it became a situation comedy that had a wide audience. Humor, mostly of a genteel type, developed from all members—adults and children. Hartmann had success with the struggles of youth, Chip and Ernie, of the earlier sitcom that had lasted twelve years. So the producer-writer created moppet twins, Buffy and Jody, plus a teenage girl, Sissy, in *Family Affair*. Vincent Terrace analyzed the qualities of characterization in this series when he wrote, "Realistically depicting children's needs and feeling, and showing that adults are capable of making mistakes, 'Family Affair' distinguishes itself from other family comedies by its heartwarming, sentimental, and at times, sad stories." (*Encyclopedia of Television Series, plots and Specials 1937-1973*, p. 147). In this reference work, the analysis seems faulty when it indicates a distinguishing realistic approach and then uses the term "sentimental," which probably should be "emotional." If this sitcom existed in the realistic mode, the work would not have an overemphasis on emotion to the point of mawkishness. There does seem to be a slight bit of a realistic treatment in *My Three Sons* and *Family Affair* that probably influenced the eventual move to such popular works as *All in the Family* and non-family works such as *M*A*S*H* and *Cheers*. Hartmann's two most popular works were at least a beginning for a situation comedy more closely related to the world as we see it.

The genesis for *Family Affair* developed with Edmund's prize-winning script, "Buffy," that aired September 12, 1966. A combined use of several types of humor might have created a popularity that ranged from the moppet to the adult audience. A teaser before the opening credits illustrated the adult appeal. Household manager French, as played by Sebastian Cabot, expresses comic exasperation as the twins, Buffy and Jody, run at bay in the apartment. Jody shoots a suction dart that lodges in the middle of French's forehead. A woman supports the wild activity by pointing out: "They mean no harm. They're just children." Cabot huffs: "Children! Madame, back home in civilization—infancy and manhood. Nothing in between." Hartmann gives the adult viewer sophisticated humor that would be worthy of playwrights Oscar Wilde or G. B. Shaw. Buffy follows the assault of her twin brother by biting French on his leg because she does not like his superior air. A switch back to a bit of slapstick. Much later Hartmann's script gives the audience a scene of genteel humor. Uncle Bill Davis (Brian Keith) talks to Buffy's doll, Mrs. Beasley, indicating that he is melting emotionally in the acceptance of her into his domain after he tries to send her off to the care of a Swiss private school. As the gentleman's gentleman for Bill Davis, Sebastian Cabot provides some of the best humor for the pilot of the series, "Buffy." As French he exhibits exasperation humor when he finds his role taking on the responsibilities of dealing with rambunctious youths. In a New York park French takes Buffy to play and meets women who have also taken children to the park. Each one is a nanny. French expresses indignation when one woman suggests that he also is a nanny. His British propriety and insistence on protocol clash with the looseness of American behavior. When all three young offspring of Bill Davis's brother become the wards of Uncle Bill, the manservant says with an appalled expression: "I am a nanny."

While many fathers in situation comedies had little relationship with a real job, space engineer Steve Douglas and the surrogate father, business consultant Bill Davis, were both wrapped up in their professions. This emphasis proved there was a movement to bring the everyday problems of being both a working parent and a father figure. The patriarchal theme continued as a creative emphasis by Hartmann with *To Rome with Love* and *The Smith Family*, two much shorter-lived series of his. John Forsythe played a college professor whose wife died and he became responsible for his three daughters. Henry Fonda as Chad Smith did have his wife, and the added burden of his duties as a plainclothesman captain for the Los Angeles police department. His profession kept him busy. However, it appears that most of the action remained off screen. *The Complete Directory to Prime Time Network and Cable TV Shows* related the nature of the work: "Stories touched on the generation gap and the problems of youth as much as on Chad's police work, which did include some dangerous situations but not really much hard action" (p. 948).

Did the trend to a realistic and social consciousness comedy such as *All in the Family* change the situation comedy series created by Hartmann? To a degree this rhetorical question has some validity. As indicated, a change in the type of family comedy already existed in the writer-producer's four sitcoms. But other forces brought the regular run of the episodes to a halt. Ed indicated that his *To Rome with Love* for CBS aired on Wednesday at 8:30 to 9:00, at the same time his *The Smith Family* appeared on the ABC Network. The name Henry Fonda carried more weight for this ABC sitcom than that of John Forsythe. Fonda knocked out Forsythe. But it becomes even more complicated than just the star status of the lead actors. Eventually *The Smith Family* would lose in its ratings. With a type of objectivity that Hartmann had about his work he said, "Who wants to look at the family life of a police officer?" Detective and cop comedies such as *Barney Miller* focused on the events in a police station. Unlike Ed's police comedy, this work realized what the audience wanted in a summer trial run and switched from a concentration on the family to Captain Barney's profession. *Barney Miller* ran for six years on ABC, the same network that aired *The Smith Family*. However, the Fonda vehicle lasted for only one season.

But there was a key change by the government body, the FCC. Ed Hartmann said this killed his shows as it did others. Prime time became by the designation of this agency to be one hour later. Instead of 7:30 p.m., the broadcast had to be 8:30 p.m. With an audience that included teenagers and moppets, the time change would lose an important segment of those who liked the family-oriented comedies. A good portion of the humor often came from the children in Hartmann's series.

Present-day evidence indicates that Ed's family sitcoms did appeal to young people. Fans of the show have established websites that show fond memories of both *My Three Sons* and *Family Affair* and want to relive their remembrances. Moppets, now grown up, reflect fondly on their enjoyment, and obvious identification with the children in the *Family Affair* series, especially Buffy, the little girl with a doll called Mrs. Beasley. Hartmann wrote the first program for this series, titled "Buffy," for which he received a best writing award. This character had some facets the writer-producer observed in his daughter, Susan Hartmann. He recalled that Susan had an imaginary friend called Mr. Beasley. Ed believed that "Mrs." would fit Buffy for this family comedy. Ironically the doll became almost as popular as the persona of *Family Affair*. Mrs. Beasley became a humorous subject for some of the programs and a doll created and sold as a special marketing item from the series became a collector's item. By 2001, thirty years after the program went off the air, the original dolls in mint condition could bring 500 dollars to a much higher price. In the October 14, 2001 *Parade Magazine,* a Sunday supplement, a firm advertised a talking doll version of Mrs. Beasley for 90 dollars. Much information on *Family Affair* appeared later on a Brian Keith website. Apparently a French woman, Michele Tirone, researched the program with the skill of a devoted fan. This series enjoyed international release and metamorphosed by translation into the language and pet names of the country. For example, the French liked "Fanfan" for the little girl, Buffy.

Both *My Three Sons* and *Family Affair* enjoyed many reruns on television. More recently *My Three Sons* had many episodes on TVland cable. The Columbia House Video Library marketed ten videotapes with a total of forty *My Three Sons* episodes. Obviously the popularity of Edmund's creations will live on. Unfortunately, Ed Hartmann has not received compensation for his considerable contributions to both the movie and television industry. His career did not last long enough into the '70s. Now, writers, directors, and actors can sometimes live on royalties for past works.

10
Rolling the Final Credits

At Edmund Hartmann's ninetieth birthday held September 8, 2001, I met his granddaughter Rachel who told me that she thought *To Rome with Love* was an excellent series. "She's the only one," Ed replied to my report of her reaction. Then with his ever-present wit that would not fade with time or age he added, "I told her to say that or she wouldn't get her inheritance."

Ed never ceased to amaze me with his jokes about the works that he developed that did not sell as well as his successes. He maintained objectivity with views on his creations seldom witnessed in movie and television industries that doted on hype and deception. He never could be bound and gagged to the stereotyped individuals in these creative worlds where illusion sometimes passed for reality.

As a political moderate, Ed proved he could give some stability to the screenwriters' organization at a time when that creative group began to recover from recriminations produced by the blacklisting. Recognized for his consensus leadership, Hartmann became the head of the Writers Guild of the West from 1955 to 1959 and the Writers Guild of America from 1960 to 1962. At this time in his career he produced significant essays. One of his most important observations appeared in the *Congressional Record*. Recognized by Senator John Tower for its evaluation and definition of our economic system, it became an important thesis marked by effective qualifications. Hartmann stressed an ethical economic system. He drew his springboard for the essay from a question posited in the 1949 musical *South Pacific*: "I know what you are against, but what are you for?" in an age that wallowed in the simplistic rhetoric of the Cold War. Early in his discussion Ed suggests the extremes of what we are against and leads into his concept of an "ethical capitalism." He states: "For 40-odd years we've been shouting that Communists are thieves, liars, cheats, and scoundrels. But a hungry, miserable world, looking for some way out of despair, isn't impressed."

Ed praised our economic system for the ability to create our country's world of plenty—so much that we have surpluses we don't know what to do with. He suggested we should be proud of our economic system without using the propaganda of the Communists. And we should be proud of our economic approach but with the ability to correct it when needed. "We should continue to welcome criticism of capitalistic flaws, scathing where justified, but in perspective" (From the *Congressional Record—Senate*, June 19, 1962, p. 10211). Originally Hartmann had created this essay entitled "But What Are You For?" which appeared in the May-June 1962 issue of *Screen Actor*.

A historian with a grasp of the period would understand how astute Hartmann's presentation would be since he qualified his stand effectively to appeal to a range of attitudes in this Cold War era. And it became obvious to historian evaluators that the '60s became a period of extensive change in social attitudes in the United States. These alterations began to be reflected in the film industry. One of the first iconoclastic movies came from director Stanley Kubrick, *Dr. Strangelove or: How I Stopped Worrying and Learned to Love the Bomb*. Released January 30, 1964, the controversy that revolved around this work became widespread. *Dr. Strangelove* could have passed if it were just an antiwar film. However, it satirized our political and military leaders. Unlike the reaction of the public, many critics praised the film. Hartmann presented an essay in a May-June 1964 *Screen Actor* entitled "Strangelove—Dissent." He became a contrary, critical iconoclast when he wrote, "The Writers Guild Film Society viewed *Dr. Strangelove* a few weeks in advance of public release. Their response was wildly enthusiastic. . . . What I am trying to figure out to my own satisfaction, is how I could be so out of step with the enthusiastic reaction." Edmund agreed with the premise of the film that nuclear fission provided a danger and error could produce a disaster. However, he questioned the idea that a future president could be a boob and military men would be "fanatic or war-hungry idiots." With this view he sided with another dissenting evaluator, *New York Times* critic Bosley Crowther. The country's questionable Vietnam engagement changed Crowther's mind. He wrote a 1977 reflection on his initial response in his book *Vintage Films* that he questioned at the time the accusation of our leaders as a "sick kind of joke." In *Vintage Films* he concluded:.

> Now I feel different about it. I feel that all this picture had to say about the phobias of warmongering generals and lies and misdeed of high officials obsessed with paranoiac fears of the "Commies," plus concern for their own images, was shockingly borne out by the behavior of our Chief Executives and our bloated defense establishment in the Vietnam War. (p. 203)

Screen Actor's editor E. T. Buck Harris pointed out in his May-June 1964 edition that while this Screen Actors Guild publication did not publish movie reviews, Hartman's evaluation needed attention. The editor welcomed his essays and was pleased with an award given for the writer-producer's article for the previous year (May-June 1963), "Sex and the Single Feature." Harris wrote a letter to Edmund on November 23, 1964, telling him that judges saw his essay as "One of the rare successful attempts at a witty feature story."

In the '60s Hollywood went boldly where they had never been before: a depiction of the sexual act. Hartmann's award-winning article poked fun at the camera moving away from a heated male-female embrace to a symbol that told the movie audience the act had been consummated. Often the visual symbol created became so abstract the viewer might have been puzzled as to what was going on. For his narration of this phenomenon in film dramas Edmund employed a Viennese psychiatrist, Dr. Alfred Schlaumer, exploring why some of his patients had recurring, disturbing mental images. Used in film were such odd symbols as the breaking of a violin string and a leaf falling from a tree. Even the cliché of the camera panning from a handy couch with the lovers on it to a fireplace with passionately burning flames. Such symbols, an interviewer tells the psychiatrist, are no longer used, and would the camera pan to a cuckoo clock?! "Yah," concluded Doktor Schlaumer, glancing at his watch. "Hollywood ist guilty." Thereby Hartmann ends the tale with a shrink convinced his patients suffer sexual frustrations from such symbolic sex.

Abstract images in the film medium became passé as the interviewer tried to get across to the Herr Doktor. In 1966 the United States Supreme Court, guided by social change and pressure from civil rights groups, swept aside much of the oppressive Production Code Seal. Hollywood could embrace a fuller range of human nature that had already been explored by the novel and stage drama in France, Britain, and the United States.

In the late '60s Ed developed an iconoclastic lampoon that developed a fascinating reversal: While the filmmakers tackled salacious themes their social gatherings moved past bawdiness to sophisticated parties. In "Decline of the Hollywood Orgy," in a November-December 1967 issue of *Screen Actor*, the satirist posits the reaction of a silent screen actor who attended a party where the shop talk concerned foreign cinema auteurs. "The consensus was that Antonioni was talented, but somewhat Fellini derivative. It was agreed that Kurosawa was superior to Bergman in composition and filmcraft." The old actor uttered a profanity that none of the guests heard—only the friend who'd brought him to the house of a dignified hostess who sported a button promoting a TV actor. The silent screen star objected to the dull event: "'The last Hollywood orgy I went to,' growled Duane, 'the only button the hostess wore was her belly button, plus spit curls and high heels'" (p. 8).

Hartmann produced two essays that satirized the new directions in the liberated storytelling of Hollywood. Again, he employed comic dissent with "The Problem as a Director Might See It" (November-December 1969) and "Decent Exposure" (March-April 1970). Both of these essays appeared in *Screen Actor*. This first article explored the frustration of a director as he urges a reluctant ingénue to take off her clothes for a soft-core sex scene. Ed's narration uses tongue in cheek by using a great deal of dialogue. This spoof dryly states: "To those directors who feel you never need a nude scene in a picture, that you can convey any message and still leave the heroine with her clothing on, all I can say is perhaps they're inhibited" (p. 5). Ed focused solely on the speech of the director with some of the humorous effect of such monologues used by stand-up comedian Bob Newhart:

You didn't realize anybody would be watching? Miss Carwell, the

Camera Operator must look at what he is photographing. No, he can't take off his glasses. I assure you the men up in the rigging are not staring down at you. They are all married men and you are just another side of beef to them. Don't cry, Miss Carwell. I just meant that they love you for your talent and your personality. They think of you as an unreachable star. . . . ." (p. 6)

Hartmann's parody in this essay indicates a type of wit that shows a growth and scope of his playwriting skills and proves innovative since he questions the trend of the times. Of course, this makes a good deal of his writing for *Screen Actor* as that of an iconoclast and satirist.

In "Decent Exposure" the title itself suggests a mockery of the trend to explore sex in the cinema—with some bitterness. He means the reverse—indecent exposure. Edmund cites a number of movies, most released in 1969. He makes pointed statements about *Midnight Cowboy, Bob & Carol & Ted & Alice, The Sterile Cuckoo, The Wild Bunch, Alice's Restaurant, On Her Majesty's Secret Service, That Cold Day in the Park,* and *Last Summer.* Hartmann does not criticize the filmmakers' right to explore the sexual nature of people. But he objects to the flippant approach of the characters in the movies to an act of love. Of *Alice's Restaurant* he wrote: [It] "is about strangers who use sex as they happen to meet, momentarily involved, as casually as traffic pausing for a traffic light." He concludes the article with, "The dirty book, adolescent idea of sex is interesting sometimes, even in a juvenile turmoil like *Hair*, but couldn't there also be an occasional adult, thoughtful treatment of sex as a grown up emotional human condition? Or has so much grace really gone out of the world?" ("Decent Exposure," p. 9). This statement indicated that the dissident writer-producer and National Chairman of the Writers Guild of America accepted the use of sex in the cinema, but he questioned the approach by quite a few filmmakers in the late '60s.

In this period one of his essays also questioned the trend of sophisticated people as they embraced pop art movies, for example, *Batman* (1966). Another essay challenged the overemphasis on youth portrayed in novels and films. The raconteur's essay on the youth fetish of the late 60s, "The Children's Crusades 1212 A.D.-1971 A.D.," employed a parallel tale of a thirteenth century shepherd boy who promises to lead his naïve followers on foot across the Mediterranean to rescue Jerusalem. It becomes a youth version of the adult trek of the time. The band of children get lost and are captured by adults and sold into slavery. Hartmann then hits home with his point in the following passages:

And as the slave traders made fortunes from the lost children of 1212 A.D. enterprising merchants cashed in on the lost children of 1971.

In Hollywood, movies made more money from reinforcing the delusions of the children than the most avid slave trader had ever dreamed.

Citing a scene from the movie without naming the film, *The Graduate* (1967), Ed related what he called the essence of the first film of this ilk showing that "all adults were fools and only the young were touched with nobility"

(*Screen Actor*, July 1971, p. 6).

Editor Buck Harris of *Screen Actor* appreciated Hartmann's essays and let him choose his own topics for his contributions. One of his most significant pieces on the art of the drama used the springboard of Hamlet's advice to the players on the purpose of acting: ". . . to hold, as 'twere, the mirror up to nature." Edmund explored the clichés by writers who use material that departs from reality. Wryly he wrote, "I have never met a spy. I have never met anyone who has met a spy. The impact of the spy in our daily life is almost nil. Yet, the ratio of spy stories to non-spy stories must place spying as our major industry." Then, again, he explored the typical tale of romance between man and woman: "I don't know of one marriage where the groom won his bride by beating up his nearest competitor. Rare fist fights among adults seldom seem to accomplish anything except clumsy and momentary satisfaction" (Both quotes from "A Question of Purpose?" p. 4).

Edmund Hartmann's most cynical and perceptive article for *Screen Actor* attacked the essence of film creativity. There has always been a different emphasis on who controlled the overall production: the writer, the producer, the director, or the actor. Drama on the stage and on the screen has always been a group art—it takes a community of people to give birth to the fiction. Editor Harris added some questions under the title, "Advice for Giants." In this August 1959 edition of his magazine, he found Ed's provocative article might make the reader wonder—"Has the Story-Teller, the Writer Become Lost in the Maze of Making a Movie? Does Hollywood Need Saving? Is the Actor in the Driver's Seat?" (p. 10). Historically, Ed traced the first person to control the screen creation as the producer, then, the director, and finally the actor. The writer, he claimed, became diminished in importance. "A writer had to write something to interest the star. It might be dull, cliché-ridden, tedious, vacuous, but if it had star quality, it was worth a fortune." Bitterly Hartmann saw the actor as one who controlled his own image and the screen drama: "Many of you new actor-managers give lip service to the Script. It is fashionable to paraphrase, 'The Play's the Thing.' The Play is not the thing at all. It is a frame for your Star image, a background, a luster about your god-like figure." Strong words and a direct attack shows the gutsy quality of the writer-producer as an essayist and evaluator. A severe analogy drives the point by a person who experienced the problem. "The movie script too often has been a chunk of meat thrown to the lions. The producer tears off a chunk; the director claws what he can get. You, the Actor, roar and snarl for the largest, bleeding bits" (p. 12).

These essays display Edmund Hartmann's gift with language that would become essential when he turned to writing for the stage. Cinema often emphasizes the visual world with occasional bursts of verbal elegance—such as the monologue Ed wrote for comedian Bob Hope in *Fancy Pants* when the leading character relates his fabricated battle with Zulu savages. Theatrical pieces thrive on the best use of words the playwright can muster.

In the '70s the entrepreneur of screen and television returned to his theatrical roots. He started in St. Louis with a college musical and moved to New York with a job in theater working for the stage tycoons, the Shuberts. Before he moved to Hollywood he contributed musical compositions for the Ziegfeld Follies and George White's Scandals. This return to the stage, of course, happened after the passing of almost forty years. His contribution featured the creation of two dramas. For Nanette Fabray, a well-known movie and television actress, he penned *The Oscar Ladies*. For Pernell Roberts, best known for his television roles in *Bonanza* and the leading, title role of *Trapper John, MD*, Ed developed the play *Welcome Home*.

In the November 16, 1972 *New York Times* the following announcement of a proposed Broadway opening appeared:

> *Welcome Home*, a first play by Edmund Hartmann, dealing with a middle-aged married man's search "for warmth and excitement," will be brought to the New York stage late in January after a test run in Chicago's Ivanhoe Theater. Pernell Roberts is starred. Joel W. Schanker and Al Manuel, coproducers, have signed George Keathley to direct.

For the Stagebill of The Ivanhoe Theatre, Hartmann commented on his play:

> In the play, *Welcome Home*, three actors play the role of Sidney Lindauer, each at a different age. Sidney Lindauer at 43 has grown into a prototype of his father, Harry Lindauer, so the same actor plays both parts.
>
> Since Sidney in his yearly years is guided and protected by his mother, he seeks out someone like her for his own wife. Therefore, Mildred Lindauer and Margaret Buckmaster are played by the same actress.
>
> Through the years from 1923 and 1954, there are always young sensual maids brought in from nearby small towns to do the housework in the Lindauer household. Each in her own way, excites Sidney's juvenile fantasies and Harry's more mature fantasies. As individuals, they differ, but as passing influences on the men, they are almost interchangeable.
>
> Someone, I think it was the lady down the street, said that life has a way of repeating itself.

Actor Pernell Roberts obviously appreciated a dual role and the challenge of playing characters of different ages. The Broadway opening of *Welcome Home,* slated for an opening the last of January 1973, never materialized. Roberts was to be replaced by William Windom, a veteran of eighteen Broadway plays and a lead in a late '60s television series *My World and Welcome to It*. Hartmann believed that Windom would have been perfect for the part but had other commitments and was not available. In Chicago the play had mixed reviews. Male journalists liked it while women critics disliked the drama. I told Ed I thought the liberation movement of women in the late '60s and the '70s may have influenced such evaluations, since he portrayed women in servants' roles, as "young sensual maids." Even if the work was a comedy it might have been considered politically incorrect, as more status by women was sought at this time. Hartmann would provide a much different emphasis in his playwriting in the late '70s. His second play, *The Oscar Ladies*, provided Ms. Fabray an exceptional feat. She had to create five different women who were nominated for the Academy Award. Nanette achieved star status for her Broadway musicals and comedian status when she replaced television actress Imogene Coca who played opposite Sid Caesar. Fabray had the background to fit the task. She exhibited the necessary versatility in her past roles and was able to handle *The Oscar Ladies*. This time the playwright moved away from Broadway to regional theatre—with performances in such major cities as Chicago, St. Louis, Cleveland, Houston, Fort Worth, San Diego, and Jacksonville, Florida. Engagements at these locations ran for twelve performances. Ed told me about the theatre in San Diego. Lawrence Welk, noted for his old-fashioned variety shows with what he called "champagne music," owned this elaborate facility. "The lobby had large pictures of Welk from the floor to the ceiling," Edmund recalled. And, of course, this indicated the inflated ego of the maestro.

This tour with Ms. Fabray proved to be tied to the times with a world that had occupied the bulk of the dramatist's career. Consequently, it became a success. While it remains only conjecture now, this work might have resulted in Hartmann capturing a Broadway success. However, the growth of regional theatre more and more made his *The Oscar Ladies* a significant victory for the growth of regional theatre across the nation.

When Ed and his wife moved to Santa Fe, New Mexico in 1992, the screenwriter and producer still formulated stage plays, so it could be said that he didn't really retire. Also, he realized that the state's tourist promoters were not wrong in the idealized pitch calling New Mexico "the Land of Enchantment." The 1990s mellowed into golden years. During our conversation February 20, 2002 he explained this period in his life:

> Being alone. Out of Hollywood. It's going to be a terribly long time. And finally you die and say goodbye to everything. Well, this is the second best time in my life. The first best was Virginia, as you know. Now I'm 90 and you'd think it was all downhill. You sit on the porch with a scarf and a rocker and you wait. Pretty soon this dark angel comes by. [Ed illustrated wings in motion with a flapping of his hands and fingers.] It's all over. I found it a world that had friends who were always there to support you. Governor Johnson recognized me as one of the treasures of the state and this society. And in recognition of past achievements in the movie arts I was given a gold bolo tie in the form of a chili.

The move to Santa Fe produced one of Edmund's surprises of his life. Virginia proved to be a wife with an instinct for the culture of New Mexico—partly because she lived in Spain for five years of her life. The state provided a multicultural land that interested her. In Santa Fe the Latino or Españo and Anglo existed as almost an equal population. In a few years Ed and Virginia found many friends. Eventually four movie critics recommended Ed for the governor's golden chili award. Three of them wrote features on his extensive background. And finally, a work by Max Wilk, as well as my evaluation biography, are books that focused on his achievements, thereby establishing his importance as a screenwriter.

Anyone examining the career of this screenwriter and movie and television producer will recognize his legacy. To be specific, his story innovation can be best illustrated by his swashbuckler, *Ali Baba and the Forty Thieves* and the detective genre, the Sherlock Holmes film, *The Scarlet Claw*—both original works of the '40s. In this same decade he created one of the best Olsen and Johnson vehicles, *Ghost Catchers*. For another the duo, Abbott and Costello, he also wrote and produced the comedy, *The Naughty Nineties*. At the end of the decade, Ed launched his first, highly successful Bob Hope movie, *The Paleface*, in 1948 and, the next year, *Sorrowful Jones*. Of the other Hope films in the '50s there were such standouts as *Fancy Pants, The Lemon Drop Kid,* and *Casanova's Big Night*. Finally, his writing and production skills were applied to long-running situation comedies for CBS television, *My Three Sons* and *Family Affair*.

One recurring reminiscence by Edmund Hartmann evolved from the many interviews. He often reflected on the temporal nature and fragility of a creator's status in Hollywood. His friendship with Preston Sturges best illustrates the fleeting nature of fame in the film capital. Ed witnessed the collapse of a creative giant of the industry. First Sturges became an outstanding writer, then writer-director of some superior movies. Some of his best were *The Lady Eve, Sullivan's Travels, The Great McGinty,* and *The Miracle of Morgan's Creek.*

Ed recalled, "I wrote an article when he died. Hollywood totally ignored it. He had no notice at all. Might have written it for *Variety*. He had bought the restaurant on Sunset Boulevard and converted it to a restaurant theatre. In his yacht he had a phone directly to the headwaiter so he could know how many people were attending. When he left Paramount he failed at RKO directing a Harold Lloyd movie. Even tried directing in France. He was busted and the government took over the dinner theatre. My wife and I were friends with Preston and his wife, who was pregnant. We were the only ones in the restaurant as the government would come and take over. All of a sudden his young, twenty-year-old wife broke into tears. He put his arm around her and said, 'Don't worry about a thing. When the last dime is gone, I'll go out on the sidewalk with a stub of a pencil and a sheet of paper and start the whole thing over again.' But he didn't."

I thought at this point of the interview how Sturges ended up "bound and gagged in Hollywood," a phrase Edmund had given me for the title of this book. I believe Sturges's fate and some of Ed's experiences shaped this cynical side of almost anyone who had become a writer for the film industry.

In this interview that related the last days of Preston Sturges the unkindest cut evolved. When Paramount CEO Y. Frank Freeman, who owed Preston $30,000, wanted another writer-director, Billy Wilder, to use him for a picture, he had the final humiliation. Wilder ridiculed him before everyone. Probably to prove he certainly remained superior to the failed writer-director.

However, good news arrived for Hartmann. Ed showed me a letter from his negotiating lawyer for a new version of Ed's situation comedy, *Family Affair*, one of his most successful creations for television. Hartmann thought the project had flown out the window—one that promised to bring him a quarter of a million. As a producer and writer for *Family Affair* Ed witnessed a run of 114 episodes on CBS. Edmund has a much higher count of the number of episodes— into the 130s. Of course, it is difficult to count all the reruns that CBS presented during the daytime from 1970 to 1973.

This interview on October 28, 2001, proved to be one of the most important and one of the concluding meetings of many sessions we had. With a pilot accepted for a September 12, 2002 airing of the new *Family Affair* on the Warner Brothers channel, his dream would be realized. The cynical side of Edmund L. Hartmann evaporated. A dramatic reversal worthy of one of the screenwriter's most optimistic films. Also, a recognition and proof of his legacy of five decades in movies, television, and the stage.

APPENDIX A

FILMS:
The majority are screenplays with some story and producer credits

Selected Leads and Important Actors

1936 *The Big Noise*	Guy Kibbee, Dick Foran, Marie Wilson
1936 *Without Orders*	Robert Armstrong, Sally Eilers
1936 *Wanted! Jane Turner* (Story)	Lee Tracy, Gloria Stuart, Judith Blake
1937 *Hideaway*	Fred Stone, Emma Dunn, Marjorie Lord
1937 *China Passage*	Constance North, Vinton Haworth
1937 *The Man Who Found Himself*	John Beal, Joan Fontaine
1937 *Behind the Headlines*	Lee Tracy, Diana Gibson
1938 *The Last Express*	Kent Taylor, Dorothea Kent, Don Brodie
1938 *Law of the Underworld*	Chester Morris, Ann Shirley
1939 *The Last Warning*	Preston Foster, Kay Linaker
1939 *Beauty for the Asking*	Lucille Ball, Patric Knowles
1939 *Ex-Champ*	Victor McLagen, Nan Grey
1939 *Two Bright Boys*	Jackie Cooper, Freddie Bartholomew
1939 *Big Time Czar*	Tom Brown, Eve Arden
1940 *Enemy Agent*	Richard Cromwell, Helen Vinson
1940 *Diamond Frontier*	Victor McLaglen, John Loder, Ann Nagel
1940 *South to Karanga*	Charles Bickford, James Craig
1940 *Ma, He's Making Eyes at Me*	Tom Brown, Constance Moore
1941 *Time Out for Rhythm*	Rudy Vallee, Ann Miller
1941 *Sweetheart of the Campus*	Ruby Keeler, Ozzie Nelson
1941 *San Francisco Docks*	Burgess Meredith, Irene Hervey

1941 *The Feminine Touch* — Rosalind Russell, Don Ameche, Kay Francis
1941 *Keep 'em Flying* (Story) — Abbott and Costello
1942 *Ride 'em Cowboy* (Story) — Abbott and Costello
1942 *Sherlock Holmes and the Secret Weapon* — Basil Rathbone, Nigel Bruce
1942 *True to the Army* — Judy Canova, Allan Jones, Ann Miller
1943 *Lady Bodyguard* — Eddie Albert, Ann Shirley
1943 *Hi 'ya, Chum* — The Ritz Brothers
1944 *Ali Baba and the Forty Thieves* — Jon Hall, Maria Montez, Turhan Bey
1944 *The Scarlet Claw* — Basil Rathbone, Nigel Bruce
1944 *Ghost Catchers* (Producer and Screenwriter) — Olsen and Johnson
1944 *In Society* (Producer and Screenwriter) — Abbott and Costello
1945 *Here Come the Co-Eds* (Story) — Abbott and Costello
1945 *Sudan* — Jon Hall, Maria Montez, Turhan Bey
1945 *Dangerous Partners* — James Craig, Signe Hasso
1945 *Naughty Nineties* (Producer and Screenwriter) — Abbott and Costello
1945 *See My Lawyer* (Producer and Screenwriter) — Olsen and Johnson
1946 *The Face of Marble* (Story) — John Carradine, Claudia Drake
1947 *Variety Girl* — (A Paramount potpourri of sketches by the company's stars)
1948 *Let's Live a Little* — Hedy Lamarr, Bob Cummings
1948 *The Paleface* — Bob Hope, Jane Russell
1949 *Sorrowful Jones* — Bob Hope, Lucille Ball
1950 *Fancy Pants* — Bob Hope, Lucille Ball
1951 *My Favorite Spy* — Bob Hope, Hedy Lamarr
1951 *The Lemon Drop Kid* — Bob Hope, Marilyn Maxwell
1953 *The Caddy* — Dean Martin and Jerry Lewis
1953 *Here Come the Girls* (Story) — Bob Hope, Rosemary Clooney
1954 *Casanova's Big Night* — Bob Hope, Joan Fontaine
1965 *The Sword of Ali Baba* — Peter Mann, Jocelyn Lane, Frank McGrath

APPENDIX B

MY THREE SONS
BROADCAST AND CAST DATA

12 Seasons, 1st and 2nd on ABC; 3rd to 12th on CBS
From September 29,1960 to August 24, 1972
Edmund L. Hartmann: Producer and Writer from 3rd to 12th Season

BASIC CAST:
Fred MacMurray .... Steve Douglas
Tim Considine (1960 to 1965) .... Mike Douglas
Stanley Livingston .... Chip Douglas
Don Grady (1960 to 1971) .... Robbie Douglas
William Frawley (1960 to 1965) .... Bub O'Casey
William Demarest (1965 to 1971) .... Charley O'Casey

Internet source TV Tome lists 380 episodes for the 12 seasons

APPENDIX C

FAMILY AFFAIR
BROADCAST AND CAST DATA
CAST DATA

5 Seasons on CBS
From September 12, 1966 to September 9, 1971
Edmund L. Hartmann created, produced, wrote, and rewrote some episodes in this series.

BASIC CAST:
Brian Keith .... Bill Davis
Sebastian Cabot .... Mr. French
John Williams (1967) .... Mr. French
Anissa Jones .... Buffy
Johnnie Whitaker .... Jody
Nancy Walker (1970-1971) .... Emily Turner

Internet source TV Tome lists 138 episodes for the 5 seasons.

APPENDIX D

FAMILY AFFAIR (2002-2003)
A WARNER BROTHERS TELEVISION BROADCAST SERIES
BROADCAST AND CAST DATA

First Season Pilot: September 12, 2002
15 Episodes for the First (and only) Season

Bob Young . . . . . Developer and Executive Producer

An experimental revival of the 1966-1971 series. Variations of some of the original CBS episodes with new plots using the same characters. Hartmann receives credit for the original story and a production credit.

BASIC CAST:
Tim Curry..Mr. Giles French
Gary Cole ....Bill Davis
Sasha Pieterse...Buffy Davis
Jimmy Pinchak ....Jody Davis
Caitlin Wachs...Sissy Davis

APPENDIX E

EARLIER SHORT RUN SERIES

TO ROME WITH LOVE*
BROADCAST AND CAST DATA

2 Seasons on CBS
From September 29, 1969 to September 21, 1971

BASIC CAST:
John Forsythe .... Michael Endicott
Joyce Menges .... Alison Endicott
Susan Neher .... Penny Endicott
Melanie Fullerton .... Mary Jane "Pokey" Endicott
Peggy Mondo .... Mama Vitale
Vito Scotti .... Gino Mancini
Gerald Michenaud .... Nico
Walter Brennan (1970-1971) .... Grandpa Andy Pruitt

This series ran for 48 episodes.

THE SMITH FAMILY*
BROADCAST AND CAST DATA

1 Season on ABC
From January 1971 to June 1972

Henry Fonda .... Detective Sergeant Chad Smith
Janet Blair .... Betty Smith
Darleen Carr .... Cindy Smith

John Carter .... Sergeant Ray Martin
Ron Howard .... Bob Smith
Michael-James Wixted .... Brian Smith
Charles McGraw .... Captain Hughes

*Both *To Rome with Love* and *The Smith Family* suffered from weak box-office ratings with the change to a dark comedy portrait of the family with the advent of *All in the Family* January 12, 1971.

SELECTED BIBLIOGRAPHY

Brooks, Tim and Earle Marsh. *The Complete Directory to Prime Time Network and Cable TV Shows: 1946-Present.* Sixth Edition, New York: Ballantine Books, 1995.
Davis, Frances. "Bob Hope, Prisoner of War," *Nation,* 30 June 2003, pp. 35-37.
Faith, William Robert. *Bob Hope: A Life of Comedy.* New York: De Capo Press, 1982, 2003.
Fantle, David and Thomas Johnson. "Bob Hope, Thanks for the Memories," *A Tribute to Bob Hope,* Golden Collectors Series, Vol. III, No. 1, London Publishing Co., 2003.
Grudens, Richard. *The Spirit of Bob Hope.* Stony Brook, New York: Celebrity Profiles Publishing, 2002.
Hanson, Patricia King, Executive Ed. *The American Film Institute Catalogue of Motion Pictures Produced in the United States Feature Films, 1941-1950.* Berkeley: University of California Press, 1999.
Hope, Bob, as told to Pete Martin. *Bob Hope's Own Story: Have Tux, Will Travel.* New York: Simon and Schuster, 2003.
Hope, Bob, with Linda Hope. *Bob Hope: My Life in Jokes.* New York: Hyperion Books, 2003.
Hope, Bob, with Melville Shavelson. *Don't Shoot, It's Only Me.* New York: G. P. Putnam's Sons, 1990.
Hope, Bob and Bob Thomas. *The Road to Hollywood.* New York: Doubleday, 1977.
Kanter, Hal. *So Far, So Funny: My Life in Show Business.* Jefferson, North Carolina: McFarland & Company, Inc., 1999.
Kliewer, Brent. "Between the Lines," *Santa Fe New Mexican* [supplement Pasatiempo] 21 May 1999, pp. 34-35.
Kroll, Jack. "Springing Eternal," *Newsweek,* 11 August 2003, pp. 62-63.
Nott, Robert. "Hartmann Videos: Mirth, Murder and Madness," *Santa Fe New Mexican* [supplement Pasatiempo], 12 August 1994, pp. 63, 68.
———. "The Kinks of Comedy: Beyond the Laughter with Veteran Screenwriter Ed Hartmann," *Filmfax,* No. 42, Dec./Jan., 1994, pp. 70-76.

———. "The Kinks of Comedy: Beyond the Laughter with Veteran Screenwriter Ed Hartmann, Part Two of an Interview by Robert Nott," *Filmfax*, No. 43, Feb./Mar. 1994, pp. 77-82, 96.
Ray, Rachel. "A candid chat with . . . Edmund Hartmann," *Santa Fean*, October 2003, pp. 86-87.
Strait, Raymond. *Bob Hope: A Tribute.* New York: Pinnacle Books, 2003.
Tucker, Ken. "Bob Hope," *Entertainment Weekly*, 8 August 2003, pp. 30, 32, 35.
Vreeland, Frank. *Foremost Films of 1938: A Yearbook of the American Screen.* New York: Pitman Publishing Corporation, 1939.

INDEX

Abbott and Costello, 1, 6-7, 10, 21, 28-29, 33-41, 42, 43, 44, 71, 90, 94
ABC Television, 80, 95, 101
Academy Awards. *See* Oscars
Adler, Felix, 38
The Adventures of Ozzie and Harriet, 63, 76, 78
The Adventures of Robin Hood, 9
The Adventures of Sherlock Holmes, 25
Ali Baba and the Forty Thieves, 9, 10, 23-24, 90, 94
Alice's Restaurant, 86
All in the Family, 30, 79, 80, 102n
Ameche, Don, 21, 28, 94
Anything Goes, 75
Arabian Nights, 22-23
Arden, Eve, 1, 76, 93
Arnold, Danny, 30, 44
At War with the Army, 44
Babes on Broadway, 22
Ball, Lucille, 1, 11, 18-19, 30, 51, 52, 53, 54, 56, 57, 93, 94
Barney Miller, 30, 80
Beauty for the Asking, 11, 18, 93
Behind the Headlines, 18, 19, 93
Bendix, William, 6
Berkeley, Martin, 71
Bernstein, Walter, 54
Bey, Turhan, 23, 24, 94
The Big Noise, 17, 93
blacklisting, vii, 69-73, 75, 83
Blair, Janet, 1, 101
Bren, J. Robert, 19
Brennan, Walter, 1, 101
Brice, Monte, 29-30

Broadway theatre, vii, 15, 28, 43, 64, 88-89
Brown, Joe E., 40
Brown, Tom, 65, 93
Brownlow, Kevin, 30
Bruce, Carol, 34-35
Bruce, Nigel, 24-25, 94
"Buttons and Bows," 49-50, 55, 61, 66
Cabot, Sebastian, 1, 2, 6, 8, 79, 97
The Caddy, 5, 30, 44-45, 94
Canova, Judy, 63-64, 94
Cantor, Eddie, 11, 27, 72
Capra, Frank, 30, 55
Carroll, Madeleine, 12, 57
Casanova's Big Night, 10, 30, 47, 58-60, 90, 94
Casey at the Bat, 29
CBS Television, 2, 6, 25, 75-76, 80, 90-91, 95, 97, 99, 101
Chamberlain, Peggy, 65
Chaney Jr., Lon, 59
Chaplin, Charles, 12, 45, 54, 70
China Passage, 18, 19, 93
Cline, Eddie, 29
Clooney, Rosemary, 62, 94
cold war, 72, 83-84
Cole, Gary, 2, 99
Cole, Nat King, 44, 72
The Colgate Comedy Hour, 75
Collins, Richard, 71
Colonna, Jerry, 64
Columbia Studios, 20, 62-63
Comedy of Terrors, 9
communists and communism, vii, 11, 29, 69-71, 73, 83-84

Cool and Lam, 25
Crime Club film series, 19
Crosby, Bing, 6, 30, 47, 55, 63, 66
Crowther, Bosley, 20, 29, 34, 49, 84
Cummings, Robert, 12-13, 94
Curry, Tim, 2, 99
Darling, W. Scott, 24
Davis, Joan, 35, 41, 64, 65
de Havilland, Olivia, 10
Demarest, William, 1, 45, 64, 78, 95
The Dentist, 48
Devine, Andy, 1, 23, 24, 65
Diamond Frontier, 19, 93
Double Indemnity, 8
Doyle, Arthur Conan, 24, 25
Dr. Strangelove, 84
Ecstasy, 11-12
Enemy Agent, 19, 93
Erickson, Leif, 23
essays by Hartmann, 83-87
Evans, Ray, 55, 61, 62, 66
Everson, William K., 25
Family Affair, 1-3, 13, 63, 78-80, 81, 90-91, 97, 99
Fancy Pants, 11, 47, 48, 50-52, 56, 87, 90, 94
Father Knows Best, 77
The Feminine Touch, 18, 21, 28, 94
Fetchit, Stepin, 16-17
Fields, W. C., 29, 37, 48
Fimberg, Hal, 29
Fine, Sylvia, 75
Finklehoffe, Freddy, 22
Fitzgerald, Ella, 35
The Fleet's In, 30
Flynn, Errol, 9-10, 65
Fonda, Henry, 1, 6, 8, 80, 101
Fontaine, Joan, 1, 10, 58, 59, 93, 94
Foran, Dick, 34-35, 93
Forsythe, John, 1, 6, 80, 101
Fox Studios, 15-17, 25
Francis, Kay, 21-22, 28, 94
Frawley, William, 1, 78, 95
Frazee, Jane, 65
Freed, Arthur, 22
Friedman, Al, 35
Fritzell, Jim, 50
Gardner, Erle Stanley, 25
Garland, Judy, 22
The Gentle Touch. See The Feminine Touch
George White's Scandals, 15, 88

Ghost Catchers, 7, 29, 35, 42-43, 90, 94
Gilbert, Billy, 23
The Gladiator, 40
The Graduate, 86
Grant, John, 28-29, 38, 41
Greenbaum, Everett, 50
Hair, 86
Hall, Jon, 1, 9, 23, 24, 94
Hammerstein, Oscar, 67
Hammett, Dashiell, 25
Hands Up, 29
Hatcher, Mary, 66
Heflin, Van, 21-22, 28
Helldorado, 17
Here Come the Co-Eds, 40-41, 94
Here Come the Girls, 30, 47, 61-62, 66, 94
Hi Diddle Diddle, 22
Hi-Hatters, 35
Hi 'ya Chum, 8, 42, 94
Hideaway, 18, 19, 93
Hilliard, Harriet. *See* Ozzie and Harriet Nelson
Hope, Bob, ix, 1, 3, 5-6, 10, 11-13, 27, 30, 45, 47-62, 66, 87, 90, 94, 103-104
Hopkins, Miriam, 63, 65
The Hound of the Baskervilles, 25
Hunt, Marsha, 69
If You Knew Susie, 27
In Society, 7, 28, 29, 33, 35, 36-37, 40, 41, 94
It's a Wonderful Life, 55
Jackson, Fred, 22
Jarrico, Paul, 71
Jivin' Jacks and Jills, 35
Jolson, Al, 72
Jones, Allan, 64-65, 94
Jumping Jacks, 44
Kanter, Hal, 5, 8, 10, 30, 52, 58, 60, 61, 62, 105
Katch, Kurt, 24
Kaye, Danny, 27, 30, 75-76
Keeler, Ruby, 37, 63, 93
Keep 'em Flying, 28, 34-35, 41, 94
Keaton, Buster, 12, 29, 30
Keith, Brian, 1, 6, 79, 81, 97
Kelly, DeForest, 66
King, Henry, 16-17
Knotts, Don, 50
Ladd, Alan, 6, 66

Index

Lahr, Bert, 75
LaMarr, Hedy, 11-12, 56, 57, 94
Lamour, Dorothy, 6, 12, 66
Lane, Rosemary 20, 29, 62
The Last Warning, 19, 93
The Lemon Drop Kid, 47, 53, 54-56, 66, 90, 94
Let's Face It, 75-76
Let's Live a Little, 12, 94
Lewis, Jerry, 1, 5, 27-28, 30, 44-45, 94
Livingston, Jay, 55, 61, 62, 66
Livingston, Stanley, 78, 95
Lloyd, Harold, 12, 33, 90
Loesser, Frank, 64, 66
Lovelace, Hunter, 15
Lowe, Edward T., 24
Lubin, Arthur, 34
Ma, He's Making Eyes at Me, 20, 64-65, 93
MacMurray, Fred, 1, 6, 8, 13, 57, 77, 78, 95
The Man from the Diner's Club, 27
The Man Who Found Himself, 18, 19, 93
Marie Galante, 16-17
Marshall, George, 50-51, 66, 72
Martin and Lewis. *See* Lewis, Jerry
Martin, Dean. *See* Lewis, Jerry
Martin, Tony, 61-62
Marx Brothers, 7, 28, 29, 42
Matthau, Walter, 54
Maxwell, Marilyn, 54-55, 56, 94
McCarthy, Joseph, 29, 70
McLeod, Norman Z., 49, 50, 52
Menjou, Adolph, 52, 53, 70
Merry Macs, 35
MGM Studios, vii, 12, 17, 21-22, 28, 47, 60, 66, 76
Miller, Ann, 20, 29, 62, 64, 93, 94
Miss Brewster's Millions, 29
Monsieur Beaucaire, 58, 59, 60
Montez, Maria, 1, 10, 11, 23, 24, 94
Moore, Constance, 65, 93
Movie Crazy, 33
movie studios. *See* Columbia Studios, Fox Studios, MGM Studios, Paramount Studios, RKO Studios, Universal Studios, Warner Brothers Studios
musicals, ix, 1, 8, 15, 20, 22, 29-30, 34-35, 37-38, 40-41, 43, 47, 61-67, 71, 75-76, 83, 87-88, 89

My Favorite Blonde, 12, 57
My Favorite Brunette, 12, 57
My Favorite Spy, 12, 30, 47, 56-57, 94
My Three Sons, 1, 8, 63, 75, 76-79, 81, 90, 95
Nash, Ogden, 21, 28
Nelson, Gene, 76
Nelson, Ozzie. *See* Ozzie and Harriet Nelson
Naughty Nineties, The, 7, 28, 29, 33-34, 35, 37-39, 41, 71, 72, 90, 94
NBC Television, 25, 75
Neslon, Ozzie. *See* Ozzie and Harriet Nelson
Never Give a Sucker an Even Break, 37
nudity, 11-12, 85-86
O'Brien, Robert, 11, 52
Olsen and Johnson, 6, 7, 8, 21, 28, 29, 35, 41, 42-44, 45, 61, 72, 90, 94
Oppenheimer, George, 21, 28
The Oscar Ladies, 88, 89
Oscars and nominations, 8, 17, 49, 61, 63, 71, 89
Ozzie and Harriet Nelson, 63. *See also The Adventures of Ozzie and Harriet, Sweethearts of the Campus*
The Paleface, 27, 47, 48-50, 52, 53, 55, 61, 66, 90, 94
Paramount Studios, vii, 6, 10, 12, 21, 47-48, 50, 52, 57, 60, 63, 66, 90, 94
Perrin, Nat, 43
Pocketful of Miracles, 30
Porter, Cole, 75-76
Pot o' Gold, 30
The Princess and the Pirate, 58, 60
Princess Nita, 15, 20
Purcell, Gertrude, 22
Qualen, John, 23
racism, 71-72, 73
Rathbone, Basil, 1, 8-9, 13, 24-25, 94
Raye, Martha, 34, 35, 41, 43, 65
Reagan, Ronald, 69-70
Restoration comedy, 21, 28
Rhythm of the Islands, 64, 65
Ride 'em Cowboy, 34, 35, 94
Ritz Brothers, 6, 7-8, 28, 29, 41-42, 94
RKO Studios, 9, 18-19, 90
The Road to Singapore, 49
Roberts, Pernell, 88
Robeson, Paul, 70, 71
Robins, Sam, 19

Rogers, Roy, 50
Roman Scandals, 11
Rooney, Mickey, 22
Rose, Jack, 48, 53
The Rose Tattoo, 30
Rubin, Stanley, 19-20
Ruggles of Red Gap, 11
Runyon, Damon, 11, 52-54, 55, 56
Russell, Jane, 27, 48, 50, 94
Russell, Rosalind, 21, 28, 94
Sailor Beware, 44
San Francisco Docks, 19, 93
The Scarlet Claw, 9, 24-25, 90, 94
Schary, Dore, 70
See My Lawyer, 7, 29, 35, 42, 43, 72, 94
Sennett, Mack, 48
The Shaggy Dog, 78
The Shakiest Gun in the West, 50
Shavelson, Melville, 53, 103
Sherlock Holmes and the Secret Weapon, 9, 24, 94
Sherlock Holmes films, 9, 24-25, 90
"Silver Bells," 55, 66
Sinatra, Frank, 63, 75
The Smith Family, 80, 101-2
Snyder, Howard, 29
Son of Paleface, 27, 48, 50, 52
Sorrowful Jones, 11, 47, 53-54, 56, 90, 94
South to Karanga, 19, 93
Sturges, Preston, 21, 90
Sudan, 24, 94
Sweetheart of the Campus, 63, 93
Sword of Ali Baba, 24, 94
Tashlin, Frank, 27-28, 48, 50
television, vii, ix, 1-2, 5-6, 8, 11, 13, 21, 25, 28, 30, 41, 44, 52, 55, 62, 63, 66, 72, 75-83, 87-91, 95-102. *See also* ABC Television, CBS Television, NBC Television, Warner Brothers Television
Temple, Shirley, 15, 52
The Thin Man (movie), 21
The Thin Man (TV series), 25
Time Out for Rhythm, 20, 29, 62-63, 64, 93
To Rome with Love, 80, 83, 101, 102n
Townsend, Leo, 71
Tracy, Lee, 18, 53, 93
Tracy, Spencer, 16-17
True to the Army, 63-64, 94

Universal Studios, 7, 9, 19, 21-25, 33-35, 37, 39, 41, 43, 61, 65, 66
Vallee, Rudy, 20, 29, 62, 93
Van Dyke, W. S., 21
Variety Girl, 6, 29, 47, 64, 65-66, 94
Virginia City, 64-65
Walker, Nancy, 1, 97
Wanted! Jane Turner, 18, 93
Warner Brothers Studios, 17, 27-28, 50
Warner Brothers Television, 2, 91, 99
Wedlock, Hugh, 29
Welcome Home, 88
White, Les, 27
Wickes, Mary, 65
Wilder, Billy, 90
Williams, Tennessee, 30, 31
Wilson, Warren, 43
Without Orders, 18, 19, 93
World War II, 9-10, 24, 34, 35, 37, 41, 44, 57, 63, 65, 71
Writers Guild, 30, 73, 83, 84, 86
Yellen, Jack, 15